I wanted children for as long as I can rer
parenting would be a wonderful experie
loving mum and my children would be e
The reality was quite different. There we
more anxiety, self-doubt, frustration, anger and upset than I thought
possible. Many times I felt despairing, not knowing what to do to
create the family life I always dreamed of. I wanted to be the best
parent I could be for my children and instead I was being the cause of
most of their unhappiness.

Several years ago I came across a philosophy that changed my life.
When applied to my parenting I saw immediate and dramatic results.
The philosophy is so simple it is almost unbelievable. The philosophy
is, "The best thing I can do for my children is be happy." I have finally
found a formula that works, every time, no exceptions.

To Anastacia,

Doing the most
important job in the
world. Keep up the
good work.

Much love   Jo x

1

Printed in the United States of America

First Printing, 2017

ISBN 978-1-9998604-0-0

Contact

easypeasyparent@gmail.com

www.easypeasyparenting.co.uk

EASY PEASY PARENTING

A Guide to Joyful Parenting

Jo Carter

CONTENTS

THE THEORY

"The purpose of our lives is to be happy."
-His Holiness, The Dalai Lama

HOW I BECAME AN EASY PEASY PARENT

"Be strong because things will get better.
It may be stormy now but it never rains forever."
-Author Unknown

I am sure many of you reading this, who are already parents, will be able to relate to my story. I wanted to have children for as long as I could remember. I met my husband at the age of twenty-four and we married within months. We tried for a honeymoon baby and we were successful. In my mind, I was going to be the best parent ever and have the best parent-child relationship I could imagine.

Everything went well until my daughter became a toddler and began to increasingly express her individuality and desire for independence. Also, I hadn't realised how my own childhood experiences and insecurities would play such a significant part in my role as Mum. Needless to say, I found parenthood to be an emotional rollercoaster and a huge learning curve.

There were lots of good times, but coupled with too many bad times for my liking. I didn't understand where I was going wrong. Like many of us, I had greatly looked forward to having children and I loved them more than life itself. So why was I screaming and shouting and sometimes even hitting this beautiful child of mine?

I often describe my eldest daughter, Rachel, as my guinea pig as she took the brunt of my learning and I have had to use the teachings in this book to help me forgive myself for the way I behaved towards her at times. I am delighted to report that, now aged twenty, she is a delightful person and we have a very close relationship. One thing I have learnt is that we are not expected to be perfect parents and that our children can thrive despite us not giving them the unconditional love we would have liked to. But parenting has the potential to be so much more enjoyable than it often is for many of us.

More children came along. Emily was born two and a half years after Rachel. Another child to care for brought a whole new set of joys and challenges. Suddenly, I was trying to meet the needs of two young children, and feeling that I was not doing the best for, not only one child, but two children, was difficult physically and emotionally. I was trying to be all things to different people and feeling overwhelmed and inadequate. Alice was born two years later, then Elizabeth two and a half years after that. John came along just over two years later, then Grace after another three years. Charlotte was born after a two and a half year gap. And finally, our latest addition, William, was born four years later.

You might be wondering why I kept having children if things were so difficult. The main reason was that there were more good times than bad, which made it all worthwhile. Also, I was a Bible-believing Christian for the first sixteen years of being a parent. There are many passages in the Bible that describe children as a blessing, and suggest that having children is a woman's main purpose and joy in life. On one occasion, I remember storming out of the living room after an upset with one of my children. I was heading for my bedroom so I could have a much-needed cry when I recalled that there was a child in my room so I wouldn't have the privacy I craved in there. I sat on the stairs crying and saying to God, "I thought children were supposed to be a blessing."

I dipped into many parenting books over the years but I found they only increased my feelings of guilt and inadequacy as I read how I should be doing things. Then a few years ago I came across a philosophy that would change mine and my children's lives forever. As I began applying these lessons to my parenting, I quickly saw improvements in my life and the children's lives. I was happier and the children were happier.

I could easily use this system. There were no complicated rules to follow, only a few basic principles. It probably sounds too good to be true yet I am living proof that this approach works.

Using the approach I am about to share with you has been like a breath of fresh air. The lessons I have learned are easy to implement and have brought joy to me and my family. There's no more need to beat yourself up or try to cram even more into your busy day or feel negative emotion without knowing what to do about it.

I believe life is meant to be good, and parenting is meant to be easy. It all hinges on how we feel. You have probably heard the adage, "If Mum isn't happy then nobody is happy." Throughout this book, I will show you tried and tested ways to increase your levels of happiness, and to use your feelings as a guidance system in order to become the best parent you can possibly be. I will also describe scenarios that will hopefully show you how you can implement the teachings into your own family life.

I have written this book in a style I would enjoy reading. It involves bite-sized chunks of information complemented by real life examples. I believe this is a perfect approach for a busy (well, less busy when you put into practise the lessons I am about to share with you) parent.

The ideas are simple yet radical; often contrary to popular culture. As you apply these nuggets of wisdom into your life you will see that they really do work and that parenting can be as joyous as you always believed.

ENJOY!

IF MUM AIN'T HAPPY THEN NOBODY IS HAPPY

"To the world you are a mother,
but to your family you are the world."
- Author unknown

What I love about this parenting approach is that, while it has a lot in common with other great parenting strategies, it is easy to remember as there is only one simple premise.

The best thing I can do for my children is be happy.

Whenever I notice that I am experiencing negative emotion, my first priority is to be happy before I do anything else.

Research from positive psychologists shows us that when we are happy, or as they would put it, *are feeling positive emotion*, we benefit in many ways. We have better health. This includes an improved immune system, reduced inflammation and reduced blood pressure. We are more creative and curious, we problem solve better, we are more resilient, so we bounce back from negative events and emotions more easily, and our outlook broadens, so we have more knowledge available to our conscious minds. When we are under stress or feeling negative emotion then our brains go into fight or flight mode and the opposite happens.

Can you imagine what a difference these benefits would make to your day to day experience as a parent? Imagine the following scenario: You are in the supermarket doing your weekly shop. A child of yours is having a bad time. They don't want to do what you want them to do and they are making a lot of noise and fuss about it. In the first instance, you are in a bad mood because of their behaviour. All sorts of thoughts are swirling around your mind (often unnoticed). Your brain and body are responding by narrowing your focus and reducing your creativity, and you decide the only option is to force your child to cooperate by means such as threats, shames, blames, and punishments. You might get the child to do what you wanted but no one is happy and your relationship is not enjoyable. In the second instance, you are still faced with a child who does not want to cooperate, but your thoughts remain positive and your brain and body stay calm and relaxed. You are coming up with creative and fun ways to help the children engage. You say yes to some of the children's requests but no to others. You are firm but fair. You are pleased with your achievement, everyone is having fun and your relationship is strengthened.

The recommendation from positive psychologists is that we make deliberate efforts to increase the number of times we experience positive emotions. They have found that when we experience a high number of positive emotions then we are able to more easily deal with the negative events and emotions that we experience.

Evidence suggests that negative experiences are beneficial as without them we would cease to grow and we would become bored. Think about lying on a beach on a tropical paradise. It would be nice for a while, but we would soon want to challenge ourselves with something new.

One aim of this book is to help us become more sensitive to negative emotion so we need only experience it for a little while before we gain the benefit from it.

Often, we are conditionally happy. That is, we are happy when things are the way we want them to be, but not happy when things are not the way we want them to be. Much of what we do as parents could be seen challenging and we can either complain or use these opportunities to practise unconditional happiness.

Many of us are waiting for our circumstances to improve in order to be happy. Maybe when the kids sleep through the night, or behave better, or pass their exams, or leave home. Often, we try to control the people or circumstances around us with our actions in an attempt to be happy. We are especially prone to doing this where our children are concerned as we often think we have the right and responsibility to do so.

The good news is that we can be happier now by becoming more unconditionally happy.

Unconditional happiness is when we are happy no matter what our circumstances are. So rather than expecting our children or our circumstances to change so we can be happy, we learn how to be happy without anyone or anything else needing to change. This is great news. *The power is in our own hands.* We can be happy now. The wonderful thing is that when we become happy we will find that our children and our circumstances will change for the better.

Being part of a family is the best place to learn unconditional happiness. If a job isn't right for you then you can change it. If a car or house isn't right then you can often change them. But changing families is much more difficult. Not many of us would want to swap our children, just improve them a little. Even this is impossible by force. That's why I believe unconditional happiness is crucial to good parenting.

As we learn how to be unconditionally happy we can help our children learn how to be happy in all circumstances. Children are mainly conditionally happy and are often unashamed in expressing their unhappiness when things are not the way they want them to be. Although it will be appropriate at times to support them in obtaining what they want, we will be of great benefit to our children if we can model unconditional happiness and teach them how to be more unconditionally happy themselves.

Often, our new thoughts will lead to new actions that increase our happiness and the happiness of those around us. We will explore this idea further throughout the book.

The rest of this book is aimed at finding ways of increasing the amount of positive emotions we have as parents. As we increase the amount of positive emotions we feel, we will be better equipped to find our own solutions as each unique situation arises.

Positive psychologists is a term describing psychologists who specialize in researching or applying what makes people, organizations or communities thrive.

USING OUR FEELINGS AS GUIDANCE

"Give your undivided attention to your job of feeling good."
-Abraham Hicks

On our journey to becoming more unconditionally happy we can use our feelings as our guidance or navigation system. Using our feeling as our guidance system is a really simple tool.

I have read many parenting books over the years looking for guidance, and I don't know about you but I have been confused by the varying and sometimes conflicting advice. When faced with a decision or a conflict I have not known what to do as I seem to forget all the good advice I have read. When we are in situations of stress we use different parts of our brain than when we are feeling creative and relaxed. In these circumstances we often resort to a fight or flight response and fall back on ways of parenting that we might have experienced which we didn't want to repeat. I presume everyone reading this book wanted children. We were probably looking forward to the joys of parenting and couldn't even imagine the downsides. While our children do bring us great joy, they often appear to be the cause of a lot of frustration, stress, anger, guilt, and exhaustion.

I believe we have the tools to be happy and parent in a joyful manner already inside us. We have simply forgotten how to use them. If we think back to our childhood, it may be that our parents or teachers weren't pleased with our behaviour at times, and might have used threats, rewards, punishments or disapproval to guide our behaviour so we learned to suppress our feelings and wants in order to receive praise or avoid disapproval. This might explain why we feel less than acceptable now and why we have forgotten how to use our guidance system, instead trying to please others.

Put simply...

When we feel bad we are moving away from what we want e.g. a happy family.

When we feel good we are moving towards what we want.

So, when we feel bad it is our main aim to feel good and we are going to look at lots of ways of doing that.

If we feel negative emotion our thoughts will normally fall into one of a few categories:

Thoughts about oneself. For example, *I am not worthy or good enough.*

Thoughts about others. For example, *They are not good enough/I don't like them/They need to be different.*

Thoughts about life. For example*, I am not safe/I am alone/I am not loved or valued/Life is supposed to be hard.*

Thoughts always come before feelings. For example, we are thinking, "I am not a very good Mum," before we feel, "Not very good." Usually we are moving so quickly through our day we don't register the thoughts and instead react to the feelings.

Also when we feel, "not very good" we think it means we are not very good.

I believe the following statement is potentially life changing. *When we feel bad it isn't because we are bad or we have done something wrong, but because we are thinking unhelpful thoughts.*

When we have thoughts that make us feel bad it is a good idea to acknowledge the thought, be appreciative of our guidance system, and find better feeling thoughts. These new thoughts might result in a different action or they might not. For example, I might be doing jobs around the house when I recognise I am feeling tired or overwhelmed. I take a few moments to think about whether this would be a good time to take a break or whether I could look at the situation differently and carry on for a while longer. I might feel better carrying on if I know people need a meal before they leave the house at a certain time but soothe myself with the promise of a leisurely bath after the work is done. I might take a break and ask someone else to take over if that is possible. I might take a break and postpone the chore if there is no hurry.

What we normally do is to feel bad about feeling bad and look for someone to blame. We will either blame ourselves or the other people involved. If we instead recognise that our unwanted feelings are caused by unhelpful thoughts we can begin looking for more helpful thoughts and let ourselves and others off the hook.

There is no need to feel bad about having bad thoughts as these will only keep you feeling bad for longer. Be easy on yourself and accept you are doing your best. Acknowledge that there are perfectly legitimate reasons for thinking and therefore feeling the way you do but that these thoughts are not serving you.

Remind yourself that you are doing well, and you are acceptable as you are. There is no pass or fail. The reward is simply to feel better, which will make your life flow better. We will discuss these concepts in more depth throughout this book.

The techniques we are going to discuss will help you to rise up the emotional scale (see The Emotional Scale). Celebrate every step in the right direction. For example, moving from a feeling of powerlessness to anger is progress and might be all one can hope for in one session. Don't stay there for too long, though. We are meant to dwell in the realms of the higher emotions, such as joy, appreciation, and love. We can think our way up there with practise.

EMOTIONAL SCALE

"Reach for the thought that feels better."
-Abraham Hicks

The techniques I will describe to you will help you move up the emotional scale. Celebrate every step in the right direction. For example, moving from a feeling of powerlessness to anger is progress. Don't plan to stay there for too long though. We are meant to dwell in the realms of the higher emotions such as joy, appreciation and love. We can think our way up there with practise.

Joy/Appreciation/Empowered/Freedom/Love
Passion
Enthusiasm/Eagerness/Happiness
Optimism
Hopefulness
Contentment
Boredom
Pessimism
Frustration/Irritation/Impatience
Overwhelmed
Disappointment
Doubt
Worry
Blame
Discouragement
Anger
Revenge
Hatred/Rage
Jealousy
Insecurity/Guilt/Unworthiness
Fear/Grief/Depression/Despair/Powerlessness

A SUGGESTED DAILY ROUTINE

"The secret of your future is hidden in your daily routine."
-Mike Murdock

Even though becoming a great parent will be easier than you might have thought, it will take time and focus. I will suggest processes you can do regularly throughout the day in order to feel good. They won't take long but they will be worth the time investment.

Start by buying an A4 notebook. Choose one you like the look of in order to enhance the pleasure of writing or journaling in it.

If possible start the day with meditation. Meditation has been proven to have a multitude of psychological and physical benefits. There are loads of resources available if you want to study meditation further. Meditation will help you to become more aware of your feelings at the early, subtle stages rather than waiting until you are in a full blown temper tantrum before trying to change how you handle a situation. You might like to simply spend ten minutes or so sitting quietly. Concentrate on your breathing and bring your attention back to that whenever you notice your mind has wandered. I also like to use guided meditations from the internet as there is rarely a moment of quiet in a household of ten people, so listening to a person's gentle instructions to breathe and relax helps me to focus. When I can, I take a walk to a local beauty spot, so I can stand there for a few minutes and gaze at lovely scenery. I usually return home feeling refreshed, which is often when insights come to me.

Following a morning's meditation I usually spend a further ten minutes or so doing one of the processes I will describe in later chapters.

I try to be realistic about what I can achieve in a day. I used to frequently underestimate what I did, and tried to fit too much in. I find that leaving plenty of scope for relaxation, doing the processes, enjoyable activities, and unforeseen occurrences, such as traffic jams, spilt milk, and a last minute nappy change, makes for a more pleasant day with much less stress.

Throughout the day I use my notebook to process any negative emotions I notice. I stop as soon as I can after the event in order to process my feelings. (I will show you how to do this in later chapters).

Before I go to bed I contemplate all the good things which have happened that day. I consider more things I can be grateful for and soothe myself regarding events I would like to have gone better (more on this later).

Be gentle with yourself. It has taken a lifetime to develop your current thought patterns so it might take a while for old habits to be replaced with new ones. At times you might think you haven't made any progress. You might go through times when a fundamental shift is occurring and it can feel unsettling to leave old ways of parenting behind when the new way isn't yet established. It is especially important to use the techniques I describe at times like these.

Imagine a car journey from one end of the country to the other. The journey could take several days. You wouldn't give up after an hour saying you had failed because you hadn't yet reached your destination. You would accept that the journey was going to take more time but celebrate that you are closer now than when you started. If you took a wrong turn you would consult your map and make every effort to get back on track again. If there were road works or a diversion you would deal with them and accept them.

Or imagine a well-worn path across a field. Hundreds of footsteps have worn away the grass to create a bare path. In a similar way your brain is riddled with neural thought pathways. As you try to find new thoughts and habits your brain will want to choose the thought pathway it is most used to. Just as the person crossing the field will want to follow the worn down path. It will take time and focus to mark out a new pathway. Writing your thought processes down will help you to focus and stay on the new path.

THE POWER OF OUR THOUGHTS

"If you think you can or think you can't, you are probable right."
- Henry Ford

WE CREATE OUR OWN REALITY

"Be careful what you think.
Your life is shaped by your thoughts."
-Holy Bible

There is a theory I subscribe to that we create our own reality. The way we think influences our lives to a greater degree than many of us realise.

Can you imagine the lives that the following two people might live?

Person A: I'm no good at anything. Nothing ever works out for me. I am a terrible parent. Life is meant to be a struggle. I can't expect to be happy when so many things are wrong with my life.

Person B: I am unique. I am beloved. I am valuable. Things always work out for me. There is no such thing as a mistake, only an opportunity to learn and grow. Life is supposed to be fun. I can find things to be happy about even if circumstances or people aren't exactly the way I want them to be right now.

Some people say that universal forces are responding to our thoughts. They might say that repeated thought patterns create a person's vibration and that vibration of energy is 'read' by Universal Intelligence, which brings you what you are thinking about. This is commonly known as the Law of Attraction, that is, like attracts like, or repeated thoughts attract real experiences to match the thoughts.

Others would dispute this but still recognise that one's attitude affects a person's life in a number of ways. An optimistic person might be more open to try out new experiences and seize opportunities. They might have a wider social network and be more proactive in seeking solutions. They might be less likely to give up and less likely to settle for less than what they really want.

If we create our own reality, then our thoughts are of ultimate importance. We do well to choose our thoughts and words carefully to match the life we want for ourselves and our children.

For the next few days, be mindful of the thoughts you think which are creating your reality.

For example, I am always so busy. I never get enough rest. The children don't help enough around the house. I always have to raise my voice to get the children to cooperate.

Consider how you could create a new reality. For example, I can choose which activities I am involved in and which I decline. I can go to bed early tonight rather than watch TV or play on the computer. I can ask my children for help. I can stay positive as I communicate with the children.

CHECK YOUR EXPLANATORY STYLE

"Optimism is the faith that leads to achievement.
Nothing can be done without hope and confidence."
-Helen Keller

In his book, *Learned Optimism, How to Change Your Mind and Your Life*, Martin E. P. Seligman. Ph.D. describes how an optimistic attitude can be learnt. He explains that everyone has a way of explaining events that happen to them. He calls this their explanatory style and the three aspects he looks at are Specific – Universal, Internal blame – External blame and Temporary – Permanent.

An optimist would generally explain an event as being specific, external, and temporary. That is, *this event will only affect specific details of my life, it is not my fault and the effects will only last for a limited period of time.*

A pessimist would generally explain an event as universal, internal, and permanent. That is, *this event will affect many aspects of my life, it is my fault, and the effects will last a long time, if not forever.*

One can imagine how an optimist or a pessimist might interpret the following events.

A child having a temper tantrum

Optimist
> Specific: *They are not happy right now.*
> External: *There is something they want that they are not getting.*
> Temporary: *They will figure this out soon / something will distract them.*

Pessimist
> Universal: They are bad-tempered.
> Internal: What have I done to make them like this?

Permanent: They will not have a good future if they carry on like this.

A child dropping and breaking a cup with milk in it

Optimist

> Specific: *Oops, a cup has been broken and milk spilled.*
> External: *That's what kids do. Accidents happen.*
> Temporary: *We can have it cleaned up in no time.*

Pessimist

> Universal: *They are always so clumsy. What a mess.*
> Internal: *Why does this always happen to me?*
> Permanent: *Will they never learn?*

Optimism isn't always the appropriate response, especially when the stakes are high and the options are risky. Optimism could lead to excessive gambling or putting oneself or others in dangerous situations. Here a healthy dose of realism would be in order. In most situations though, keeping a positive mental attitude will increase the amount of positive emotions, help reduce anxiety and low self-esteem, and ultimately create better life circumstances.

Use your journal to record thought patterns that you notice throughout the day. Are they optimistic or pessimistic?

NEGATIVE TO POSITIVE THOUGHTS

"Change your thoughts and you change your world."
-Norman Vincent Peale

Another process that works beautifully to improve my mood is to find positive thoughts to counteract any negative thoughts I might be having.

Imagine a path that has been formed across a field by you walking the same route day after day. The grass has stopped growing and instead the path is just brown soil. Imagine that this well-worn path represents a thought habit that isn't serving you. That is, thinking the thought makes you feel bad. In creating a new thought habit that makes you feel better we are attempting to create a new path across the field. Initially it will take concentration to walk on the new route and avoid the well-worn path. Lack of focus will cause us to walk along the familiar well-worn path. Similarly, adverse conditions such as wind, rain, fog or the blackness of night, which might represent difficult circumstances or people or hunger or tiredness, could easily cause to slip onto the old path. Don't despair when this happens. As soon as you recognise what has happened simply choose to use the new path again. As we consciously choose to use the new path it will become more worn and therefore easier to find and follow. The old path will grow over because of lack of use. The new path will become your habitual route.

Recently I asked my husband to join the children and I at a local park. The children and I enjoy our time together but we love having Dad with us as well. He is often busy at work and he is very industrious at home so this was a rare treat. We have been married twenty years and I can honestly say that he has only been to the park with us a handful of times.

The day started off very sunny but by the time my hardworking husband had cleaned the car and I had made an impromptu visit to a relative in hospital, the weather had turned decidedly dull. By the time we arrived at the park we could feel the odd raindrop, which rapidly turned into light rain, and within half an hour it had turned into a downpour.

In the past I would have felt very sorry for myself, looking for someone to blame for how the day turned out. It would then have been my mood that would have spoiled the day, not the weather.

So the thoughts I might have had are:
> Why did he have to clean the car?
> Doesn't he care about spending time with us?
> He doesn't love us.
> I am so upset that we can't have this fun time together.

Instead I chose to think:
> I am so glad that he decided to come with us.
> We had half an hour together.
> It was fun running back to the car in the rain.
> Now that my husband has seen how much fun we can have he might be inclined to come out with us more often.
> We can continue the fun with card or board games at home as we have set this time aside for fun.
> This is a great opportunity to show the children how to be unconditionally happy.

On another occasion I went into my three year old daughter's room to wake her only to find that she had vomited in the night. She was fine and happily played in the bath while I cleaned the bed sheets. I was appreciative of the fact that I had used a waterproof mattress cover to protect the bed, I was appreciative of my washing machine and the fact it was good drying weather.

Later in the day the same daughter had eaten a chocolate ice lolly on my bed and managed to get chocolate all over the covers. This time it was more difficult to stay positive as I thought she couldn't help vomiting but should have known not to eat a chocolate ice lolly on my bed (I always ask the children to eat at the dining table). I managed to stay cheerful by telling myself she is only little and it will only take a few minutes to clear up. The washing machine and good drying weather were still available.

ABCDE METHOD

"It is not things themselves that trouble us but our opinion of things."
-Epictetus

You might find it more useful to do the previous process in a more structured way. The method I have discovered in Martin Seligman's book, *Learned Optimism*, is what I call, the ABCDE method. I find it easy to remember and very powerful.

A = Adversity. What has happened that has activated negative thoughts? What do I feel has gone wrong?

B = Belief. What negative thoughts am I thinking about the event?

C = Consequences. How do these beliefs make me feel?

D = Disputation. In this section one challenges the beliefs by looking at the evidence for the belief and questioning its validity and by looking for alternative explanations.

E = Energization. How do I feel now that I have disputed my original beliefs?

This process works well for a number of reasons. Firstly, we are focusing on the fact that it is not the event or circumstance or person that causes our negative emotions but rather the thoughts and beliefs we hold about the event or circumstance or person. Secondly, in writing all our thoughts down we are helping to untangle our thoughts and uncovering thoughts and beliefs we didn't even realise we had, which are causing us unnecessary suffering. Thirdly, the process makes us more conscious of the link between our thoughts and our feelings and the power we have to control our thoughts and therefore our feelings.

Now for some examples:

Adversity. I am a full time mum and although I love having children of all ages in the house I sometimes feel held back from doing other things I want to do. I want to travel, write, attend parties, live abroad.

Belief. I can't have it all.

Consequences. I feel frustrated and trapped at times.

Disputation. I can have the essence of what I want in my current circumstances.
There is great potential for fun with so many children in the house.
We can have parties here.
With a capable and willing nineteen year old daughter at home I can attend the odd party and my children will be well looked after at home.
My family are my stabilizing force. Without them I might have emigrated and not enjoyed living abroad as much as I think I would.
Travelling and parties and more writing can be a part of my experience in the future.
I do have time to write now. My family experiences give me material to write about.
I do go to the theatre and cinema and parties on occasion.
I appreciate my family so much.
Appreciating everything in my life now makes me happy.
Get happy and then see how I am inspired to act, if at all.
Sometimes a change in perspective is all that is needed.
Sometimes action will be inspired but it will come easily as I get happy.

Energization. I feel much calmer. I feel great love for my family and appreciation for my current lifestyle.

Here is another example:

Adversity. A child has spilled some milk just as we are about to leave the house in a rush.

Belief. My child is clumsy and careless. I don't like to waste things. If I clean it up now we will be late yet I don't want to leave a mess. Now I have more work to do and I already overwhelmed.

Consequences. I feel stressed, worried and angry. I am in fight or flight mode and my problem solving capacity is limited.

Disputation. Accidents can happen to anyone. Children are still learning motor skills. It is what it is (and no use crying over). Milk doesn't cost much. I can throw a cloth over the milk now and clean it up properly later. It will only take a few minutes. This can serve as a reminder that I need to plan to leave the house in plenty of time so that I can deal calmly with unexpected events.

Energization. I feel calmer and more loving toward my child.

The next time you experience negative emotion make every effort to use the ABCDE process. Use your journal to analyse what your thought processes were and how you could find new better feeling thoughts.

ABCDE PROCESS IN PRACTISE

"There are no mistakes or failures, only lessons."
-Denis Waitley

A production company contacted me recently asking me to send them a video of myself answering questions about who should be prioritized in the family. There were several attempts before I had material that would be good enough to send. I had asked the children to stay out of my bedroom while I filmed but my four year old was becoming restless so decided to enter the room just as I was in the middle of answering a question. I thought I had turned the camera off then proceeded to tell her off for disturbing me. I sent the video but on watching it back saw the footage of me reprimanding my daughter. I had forgotten it was on the recording. I felt embarrassed and worried. This was a perfect opportunity to use the ABCDE technique.

Adversity. I have sent a video of myself to a production company showing me reprimanding my daughter.

Belief. They are going to think that I am a terrible parent. They might not want to feature me on their show. I shouldn't have told her off. I am not a good parent.

Consequence. I feel embarrassed and worried about the outcome and irritated at Charlotte.

Disputation. I don't claim to be a perfect parent. In fact, this is a perfect opportunity to practise what I preach. Charlotte had been clearly told not to come upstairs so I wasn't wrong to firmly remind her. Charlotte wasn't upset. Charlotte is only young so it must have been difficult for her to be patient. She may have genuinely forgotten. I know that the best thing I can do for my family is to feel good so I choose to give myself the benefit of the doubt.

Energised. What felt like a mistake feels like a learning experience.

FIND BETTER FEELING THOUGHTS

"Happiness is a journey, not a destination."
-Alfred D'Souza

When I am being less than I want to be and less than I know I can be it is easy to think that I have forgotten everything and made no progress on the path to more joyful parenting.

Having given birth to my eighth baby the day before, I was feeling tired and irritable and found myself raising my voice to my adorable children who were making too much noise for my liking and ignoring my requests to be left alone while I slept.

I was hoping and expecting that the first few days after my son's birth would be filled with beautiful moments to be treasured as we had all been looking forward to his arrival so much. This expectation made me feel more disappointed in myself than if it had been just another ordinary day.

In that moment it felt as though I would always lean towards grumpiness and I would never be the unconditionally joyful, loving parent I wished to be.

The difference this time was that as I recognised my negative thoughts I knew what to do!

So I decided to find the best feeling thoughts that I could. (The children were still interrupting me so I couldn't rely on my circumstances to make me happy, and my husband was equally as tired and irritable so I couldn't look to him to cheer me up.) I decided I wanted to feel good even more than I wanted to be left alone. Recognising that I had the power to change my mood in this circumstance was so exciting for me and I immediately took the easy steps of finding better feeling thoughts.

Better feeling thoughts about me included: *I have just had a baby and I am exhausted. It is no wonder I am feeling irritable; beating myself up will not help but forgiving myself and allowing myself to be human will help me to feel better sooner; no one is perfect; the children will survive a little bit of grumpiness from me; this is another opportunity for them to stay in touch with their own guidance system; we have enough lovely interactions to counteract these negative interactions; I remember what it is like to feel good about myself and others and I will feel that way again very soon; this will not last; I will feel better after a sleep.*

I also found better feeling thoughts about my children: *They are just excited; they are young and not mature enough to be considering my feelings at all times; they aren't being deliberately disobedient; they will have asked their questions and found something to amuse themselves soon enough; I love them all so much.*

I decided to spend time thinking positively about my husband in anticipation of our next interaction: *Bill is feeling tired and overwhelmed with looking after us all; he has had a few busy days at work and a few nights of broken sleep; he is doing his best; I wouldn't like someone pointing out my grumpiness to me so I won't do it to him as it doesn't help; he is doing a good job of organizing the family and keeping the home in order; I don't need him to be in a good mood in order for me to be happy; this is a great opportunity for me to practise unconditional happiness.*

I felt better straight away. The kids eventually drifted off to be involved in their own activities and I got my desired sleep.

It takes practise to consistently find better feeling thoughts. Old thoughts of needing to be a perfect parent will raise their head from time to time. Each time we recognise unhelpful thought patterns and replace them with new, better feeling thoughts we are treading a new path that will eventually become our new habits of thought.

I was slowly but surely creating a new path of thoughts. It was becoming easier and easier as I practised finding better feeling thoughts. If I did forget it was no big deal as I could easily get back into alignment and feel good.

Don't give up.

You are an ever-evolving being.

You can create a new reality for you and your family.

GREAT EXPECTATIONS

"Happiness is an inside job."
-William Arthur Ward

Wouldn't life be easier if everyone behaved in a way that pleased us? Many of us, without realising it, need other people's behaviour to be a certain way before we can be happy. The problem with this approach is that we give all our power away. The good news is we can be happy despite what is going on around us. When we find ways to make ourselves happy we often find that other people's behaviour changes for the better.

Let me give you an example. Christmas Day is often a day of high expectations, and our home was no different. We have a tradition of taking it in turns to open our presents while everyone else pays attention to see what we have received, sharing our joy. The family was sat together in the lounge opening our Christmas presents. One of my children was upset because people were chatting as she was opening one of her presents. Another child then got upset because she felt the behaviour and mood of the first child was, "spoiling everything." I was tempted to be upset at both children but realised I would be doing exactly what they were both doing, that is, letting another person's behaviour upset me. I soothed myself with thoughts such as, "Expectations are unnaturally high at Christmas," and, "She will be distracted and feel better soon," and, "The best thing I can do is pay no attention to their upset but instead find things to be happy about." The incident blew over in seconds and everyone was soon enjoying themselves again.

My recent birthday was another occasion when I had to remind myself this was just another day. The trouble started at the dinner table. The younger children and I had enjoyed a day with friends and we all enjoyed the grand opening of cards and presents when my husband came home from work and my mum arrived for dinner. The children were looking forward to helping me eat my birthday chocolates. My eighteen year old, Emily, was responsible for making the evening meals for one week only as she was on half term from college and her sister, who usually made the evening meal, was away. I had given Emily instructions regarding dinner, which was to be a cook-in-sauce chicken dish, but she had left the preparations too late to follow the instructions on the jar so decided to fry the chicken and add the warmed sauce just before serving. Her dad and I were disappointed that the chicken seemed undercooked and the sauce didn't taste right. Emily was upset due to feeling unappreciated. Everyone left the dinner table in a bad mood.

It was only the day after when I realised I would rather be happy than right. Yes, Emily could have followed instructions more carefully but I could have explained them better. Yes, the chicken hadn't turned out as hoped but she had used her initiative. I decided to focus on the positives in the situation and remember that I am responsible for my own happiness. Emily is learning that sulking about performing a chore does not mean she is excused from it. Learning to be happy even when circumstances aren't exactly the way we want them is the recipe for a great life.

NEEDING CIRCUMSTANCES TO BE PERFECT IN ORDER TO BE HAPPY

"Always remember, your focus determines your reality."
-George Lucas

Unless I take control of my thoughts and my feelings I will always demand more and more in order to feel good.

Having been practising doing more of what I wanted to do and less of what I felt I should be doing, I found the house was becoming cleaner and tidier. I was also valuing my role and learning to ask for help earlier rather than waiting until I felt overwhelmed (more on this later). The only problem was I was so pleased at how the house looked that I started looking to that condition in order to feel happy.

In the past I would have been okay with a certain level of 'mess.' I would tell myself that it was inevitable that the house would be less than perfect with so many people living in it. As long as I could find things when I needed them, I would be okay with some mess.

Now the house was cleaner and tidier I was expecting no more moments of stress and no more shouting at the kids to clean and tidy after themselves. Instead I was still being more conditionally happy than I realised. My expectations had raised and I was shouting at my children when the state of the house had fallen below my new acceptable standard.

I was focusing on the things that were 'wrong' rather than focusing on all the things that were working well. One cup left out was annoying to me whereas in the past it would have taken three cups left in my teenage daughter's room to aggravate me.

I, as much as anyone, appreciate pleasing conditions. I appreciate a bright spring day or the warm summer sun or driving when the traffic is flowing or helpful children or relaxing in the steam room but it is so easy to become so used to these pleasant conditions that we feel less than appreciative when the conditions are not perfect.

It was my birthday a few days ago and my husband and I met at the local gym after work to have a swim followed by a chat in the steam room. We hadn't been to the gym together for a while as Bill had been ill. When we arrived at the pool we realised that the steam room was being cleaned so was out of use. My heart sank a little until the lovely cleaner reassured me that they would be finished soon and the room would be hot again in 10 minutes or so. The cleaning was finished and I eagerly anticipated the steam room being ready. Then the electrician arrived to change some light fittings and I knew that any hope of a steam that day was over.

The above incident may sound trivial but it served to remind me of how marvellous my life really was. I have a loving husband, eight happy and healthy children and a life full of enjoyable things. Yet here I was, being tempted to sulk because the steam room was out of order. I was thankful of the reminder to be unconditionally happy.

LOVING OURSELVES

"If we can't love ourselves,
how the hell are we gonna love anybody else?"
-RuPaul Charles

SEEKING VALIDATION

"No matter what anybody says,
what matters most is what you think of yourself."
-India Arie

I was a good student. I always worked hard and did well at exams. Prior to having children I qualified as a midwife. I only worked for a year but I was glad to tell people I was a midwife because answering with, "I'm a Mum" didn't impress anyone when they asked what I did. Having a qualification meant people knew how to categorize me and it gave me some value in their eyes.

I remember bumping into a teacher who had taught me when I was in high school. He was surprised I had chosen to be a stay-at-home mum because he felt I was intelligent and my talents were not being fully utilized unless I had a career. I am not for one minute suggesting that being a full time mum is preferable to being a working mum. I have huge admiration for mums who also work outside the home (or from home). The point I am making is that being a full time mum is often undervalued by society.

Having received praise and feedback in the form of grades and qualifications all through my school and college years, and then during my midwifery studies, I floundered without the positive feedback from others, especially when I felt unsure of how I was performing in my role as Mum. What was the test I needed to past? How did I know if I was doing motherhood right? No one was giving me regular reviews of my performance, and I now realise that I set unrealistically high standards for myself. I was destined to fail by my own standards. Constant self-criticism meant that I magnified the times I lost my temper or spoke unkindly to the children, and I didn't give myself enough credit for all the happy times I helped to create or the small achievements. Needless to say, my self-esteem was pretty low at times.

Studying for a counselling qualification years later helped me understand that I was, like many people, externally validated. I understand external validation to mean looking to others for approval or for a sense of who I am. I struggled to feel good without the regular input from others in the form of good exam results or positive feedback from my work as a midwife. My work was to become internally validated and approve of myself.

THE IMPORTANCE OF SELF-TALK

"Be careful how you talk to yourself because you are listening."
-Lisa M. Hayes

In order to become internally validated we need to practise approving of ourselves and listening to our own guidance system rather than trying to please others in order to get their approval.

Imagine somebody following you around all day, criticizing what you do and calling you names. You wouldn't tolerate it yet we do this to ourselves all the time. We focus on what we have done 'wrong,' and what we 'should' have done. We mistakenly think we will become better if we point out our faults to ourselves, but in fact we only end up feeling bad, and the cycle continues.

I believe we are all perfect as we are. If you had a £1 coin that was discoloured and dirty it would still be worth £1. I believe that even though we sometimes think and act in ways that we would rather not, that doesn't mean we are of any less value than a perfect human being. We have all got baggage. We are all doing our best. This is helpful to remember when someone is behaving towards us in a way that we don't like. We are all doing our best with the knowledge and beliefs that we have. NO ONE IS PERFECT so beating myself up is unnecessary and unhelpful.

When we remember we are acceptable as we are, transformation happens and we become a better version of ourselves. We often try to do it the other way around. That is, *I will accept myself when I have got control of my anger or when I'm kinder or less selfish, more talented, more productive, more worthwhile, but until then I'm going to speak harshly to myself.* So, when we get angry, have an unkind thought, over-indulge in junk food, and so on, we feel terrible for it. Guilt and shame are not conducive to personal growth. Self-love and acceptance help us to continue with hope and joy.

Criticism causes our body to release the stress inducing hormones of Adrenaline and Cortisole. These hormones are useful if we need to outrun a wild animal but not conducive to rational, loving parenting. Compassion causes us to release Oxytocin and Opiates, feel-good chemicals that put is in the optimal mind-set to do our best.

What critical statements do we commonly say to ourselves?

'I am doing a rubbish job.' 'I am always losing my temper.' 'I bet none of my friends behave like this towards their children.'

What compassionate statements could we make instead?

'I was tired, overwhelmed, felt unappreciated.' 'There is no such thing as a perfect parent.' 'I am doing my best.'

LOVE BUILDS US UP

*"You yourself, as much as anybody in the entire universe,
deserve your love and affection."*
-Buddha

Many of us value ourselves by comparing ourselves to others and I was no different.

If I was feeling that my parenting wasn't good enough I might feel a little better if I saw another parent struggling to cope with their children as I could compare myself favourably to them. If I noticed a parent whose approach seemed better than mine I would feel even worse as I compared myself to them.

If I was feeling good about myself and confident in my parenting abilities at the time I would feel compassion for the struggling mum and hope to learn from the mum whose parenting I admired.

Why do we value ourselves in this way? Our society and education system often compares us to one another and grades us accordingly. Maybe our parents or teachers or other caregivers celebrated our talents and criticised us when our behaviour didn't please them. Maybe, because as a society we praise academic intelligence or certain physical attributes, we allow ourselves to feel good or bad according to how we measure up to society's standards. Maybe our religious upbringing has instilled in us the belief that we are less than perfect. Whatever the reason, I am sure these are harmful and unnecessary.

When we realise our value isn't dependant on how we measure up or compare to others, we can enjoy our talents without feeling superior to others, and we can appreciate other's unique gifts without having to feel inferior. We can recognise our individual strengths, qualities, and gifts. We can celebrate them, use them, and develop them, and appreciate the fact that we all have some part to play in the grand scheme of life, but we don't have to be the whole part. Let someone else play their part without feeling inferior. We can rejoice in someone else's unique talents, personality type, and perspective because it doesn't affect our value at all.

A favourite phrase of mine is, "We're all doing our best." Now when I see a parent or a child in a bad mood, rather than judge them or compare myself to them I recognise they are feeling bad at that moment. Realising that no one is perfect helps me to give myself and others a break.

TRYING TO CONTROL THE UNCONTROLLABLE

*"If we could look into each other's hearts,
and understand the unique challenges each of us faces,
I think we would treat each other much more gently,
with more love, patience, tolerance and care."*
-Marvin J. Ashton

I had been feeling frustrated with my own mum. I felt she should be different than she was. I wanted a mum who would help more with the children, be more supportive and encouraging of my efforts and achievements. I wanted my mum to be more light hearted and positive.

These feelings were stronger than ever before. I found this confusing as I knew that my aim was unconditional happiness and I had been doing well with other aspects of my life. I have since realised that using these processes helps to release previously unrecognised limiting beliefs. I was just noticing the belief so I could address it.

I had been pondering these negative feelings about my mum when I was met with unrealistic expectations from my own child. My eldest daughter Rachel was visiting for a few days. We had spent a lot of time over the weekend chatting about her life at University and we were getting on well.

We were going to a local restaurant to have a meal to celebrate my second daughter's eighteenth birthday. As we entered, Rachel was chatting to me about something but I wasn't really paying attention as I was focusing on seating our group of eleven. Rachel was upset that I hadn't given her a comprehensive reply. I was really upset and annoyed. How dare she demand so much of me? I had given her a lot of attention over the weekend. Couldn't she see how busy I was?

I couldn't enjoy the rest of the evening fully as I was hurt by my daughter's criticism. I recognised immediately that the feelings my daughter was having towards me were a reflection of the feelings I was having towards my own mum. I knew I would work it out eventually but I needed quiet time to process my thoughts and feelings.

My goal was to feel better. I could see that my intentions were always good and that I always did my best but my best wouldn't be good enough for all of the people all of the time. That was something they would have to deal with. As I recognised that I was doing my best I could recognise that my mum was also doing her best and she has no obligation to be or do anything for me. It is my responsibility to be happy by looking at her positive qualities just as my daughter could be happy by focusing on my positive qualities.

A LESS THAN PERFECT PARENT

"Why do I expect from myself
what no one else has managed to achieve?"
-Jo Carter

I have found that many parents have such high expectations of themselves that they easily feel self-critical. We beat ourselves up for being less than perfect. We regret the 'damage' we perceive we are doing or have done to our children. We love our children so much and want the best for them yet we feel powerless to be the parent we want to be. It is often the parents with the highest standards who feel the most negative emotion as they fail to meet those standards.

What is to be done? My ponderings have led me to the conclusion that parents can't be expected to be perfect before we are entrusted with these precious lives to care for because, let's face it, no one is. When we understand the importance of 'contrast' for us and for our children we will find it easier to forgive ourselves and be satisfied that we are doing our best at the time. So what is contrast?

Contrast is anything we experience that is unwanted.

We make the mistake of thinking contrast isn't good for us when, in fact, contrast is unavoidable for us and our children and it can bring us great benefit if we know what to do with it.

I find that my periods of greatest growth are the times when I have experienced a lot of contrast. I expect we can all look back and think of a time in our lives which we didn't enjoy going through, but that has been the cause of substantial personal growth.

Contrast will come into our children's lives because of us (for example, experiencing Mum or Dad in a bad mood might not be pleasant) and it will do them no ultimate harm as they learn to look to themselves for their sense of value rather than to us. Also, they can learn how to be happy even when those around them are not happy.

We do our children no favours if we strive to overprotect them from naturally occurring contrast.

As we model our increasing ability to be unconditionally happy we can help our children gain the same skills that will serve them extremely well throughout their lives.

MIND YOUR OWN BUSINESS

"Setting an example is not the main means of influencing another,
It is the only means."
-Albert Einstein

Families come in all shapes and sizes and blended families are increasingly common.

A young mum whom I shall call Sue recently came to me for advice. She was wondering how to influence a child that she only had custody for a few days a week. Sue was in a relationship with the child's father and relations with his ex-partner, the child's mum were strained to say the least. Sue was worried that any approach she used was contradicted by the child's mum. To complicate matters further, Sue and her partner, whom I shall call Sam, lived with Sam's parents. They also had an opinion of how the child should be raised.

I advised Sue to be concerned only with her own mood and relationship with the child and not worry about how the other family members related to Sue. Sue was to keep positive by focusing on the positive aspects of all the people involved in the child's life. She was to give them the benefit of the doubt and not to 'bad mouth' the other family members especially around the child.

This might seem overly simplistic but have you ever noticed how children behave differently depending on who is around? On the odd occasion I have left my children with Grandma for an hour or two, I am often greeted by unhappy children. Grandma informs me that the children have been playing beautifully all afternoon and only started to argue and complain on my return. I have witnessed this phenomenon myself when looking after friend's children. They are polite, kind and cooperative for me but seem to have a personality change the minute my friend arrives.

I would go so far as to say, do not become involved in the relationship between the children and your partner, unless you are genuinely concerned for the child's wellbeing. Each member of the family is responsible for his or her own happiness and their relationship with others. It is not my job to micromanage all the relationships in my family. Instead, I put all my efforts into unconditionally loving all the members individually. So if I hear my husband and a child arguing I do not rush in to referee or stop an argument. If there has been a disagreement I can offer support after the event if it is requested. From this general place of loving rather than judging I can help either party have compassion for themselves and the other person involved.

Returning to the subject of Sue, children are very adaptable and will modify their behaviour to suit different circumstances and different people. Sue's chief benefit to the child she cares so much about is to be as unconditionally happy as possible while the child is with her. The close relationship that she can potentially build with that child can help the child cope with other, more difficult relationships. The child will see how Sue attempts to love rather than hate, and give the benefit of the doubt rather than judge. The child will see how Sue is happy and in wanting to be happy herself, is more likely to model Sue's attitude than the attitude of others that she comes into contact with.

Although we would dearly love for our children to be surrounded by unconditionally loving and happy people all the time, that is never going to happen. We need to remember that we are sometimes 'the bad guy'. We help our child enormously as we show them how to forgive ourselves and others.

OVERCOMING NEGATIVITY BIAS

"Our negative experiences stick to us like Velcro,
While our positive experiences slide off us like Teflon."
-Dr. Rick Hanson

Many of us are negatively biased, which means we tend to focus on and remember what has gone wrong rather than what has gone well. Many times I will ruminate about the one time I spoke to my child harshly during the day rather than focusing on all the fun interactions we had that day.

We believe that focusing on our faults will help us improve but it discourages us instead. This isn't beneficial in helping us become the parents we desire to be.

In order to counteract negativity bias, think back to today or yesterday and try to remember at least three things that went well.

Maybe a potentially difficult situation was handled well. Did you have any fun times with your children? Have you done anything you enjoyed today?

As you try to recall things that went well you might find instances you would rather forget spring to mind instead. When this happens remind yourself that you are a work in progress, that you are doing your best, and that the easiest way to become the parent you would really like to be is to show yourself compassion for where you are.

NO ONE IS PERFECT

"The injunction that we should love our neighbours as ourselves means that we should love ourselves as we love our neighbours."
-Nicolas Chamfort

The combination of being raised in a critical household and my religious upbringing meant my inner voice was a mish-mash of my mother's voice and a stern God who might punish me if I made a mistake. This led me to setting impossibly high standards for myself in order to gain my mum's or God's approval. When I felt good I could imagine God speaking kindly to me, but when I had lost my temper or had done something else I regretted I always felt God was displeased with me.

One day, I remember blowing my top with the kids and throwing myself onto my bed. I was fuming, and I felt horrible inside, like the parts of my personality that were normally under control had taken over. I couldn't recognise anything good in me. At times like this I would feel unworthy of talking to God and I would fume and feel terrible, until eventually I would forget the experience and carry on. Then I would start talking to God again and hope He hadn't noticed. One day I must have had enough of this pattern because after one particularly fierce episode, almost shouting to God, "Go on then, love me now?" a huge sense of peace and love swept over me and I could see the illogic of thinking that I was loveable only when I was behaving well. During the times that I felt unlovable, I needed love the most. That was a real turning point for me and I started to accept myself, warts and all.

Since this angry episode I have learned to listen to those parts of my personality that I had tried to suppress in the past. I have learned to respect them and express them in a way that doesn't hurt people. For example, I had the belief that a mother should always put her children first, especially a Christian mother. This led to me feeling a lot of resentment and pent-up anger. From listening to my angry thoughts, I have learnt that I do need to take a break at times, it's okay to say no, and I can have fun even if the children aren't sharing the experience with me. I don't have to sacrifice my own wants and needs for my children. You might recognise the same experiences in your own life. You may have different symptoms, such as sadness rather than anger if you are not acknowledging a part of your personality that wants to be heard.

YOU ARE ENOUGH

"Accept everything about yourself,
I mean everything.
You are you and that is the beginning and the end.
No apologies, no regrets."
-Clark Moustakas

It is worth noting that we might experience what we consider setbacks during our parenting journey. I had been thoroughly enjoying my time with my children and thought all my troubles were over when the following incident occurred:

I had been thinking about how we value ourselves in our society and how I value myself. Having been, "Just a mum" for the last twenty years in a society that increasingly undervalues the role of parents, I realised that most of my struggles concerning self-esteem had been down to not realising my inherent, unconditional value. My value was tied up with my role as a mum. This was all well and good when the house was clean and tidy, nutritious food was regularly served from my kitchen, and the children were happy and appreciative, but when the children were having a bad day or the house was a mess or we had beans and toast for tea, I was hard on myself thinking, *What have I got to be proud of?* Whilst I have learned to take time for myself and speak kindly to myself, recognising that no one is perfect and that my needs are as important as the children's, I learned that feeling less than worthy was still an issue for me.

I had been journaling that I wanted to truly KNOW my value, and I thought I would wake up one morning feeling inherently valuable. In reality, ten days of weeping and angry outbursts was followed by guilt and further weeping as I got in touch with painful feelings that I was 'not enough.' From that place of feeling empty handed, with nothing to show to impress someone who was looking for reasons to value me, I finally realised, 'Here I am, at my worst and I am still valuable.' What a relief! I could stop trying to impress whoever I was trying to impress. (For some it might be a deity or a parent or a lover or a peer group.)

During the period of time I was feeling out of sorts I thought I had forgotten everything and I couldn't understand what was happening. After the event I could see this was just another part of my learning journey and that nothing had gone wrong. When we stop striving to become worthy or valuable we can recognise our inherent value and become a better, happier version of ourselves.

HOW PEOPLE TREAT YOU IS AN INDICATION OF HOW YOU FEEL ABOUT YOURSELF

"How people treat you is an indication of how you feel about yourself"
-Abraham Hicks

I had a two-week old baby, and I'd needed a blood transfusion after the birth so had been advised to take things easy. This definitely fitted in with my philosophy of doing more of what you want rather than what you feel you should do, so I was happy to agree. The only trouble was, my husband was feeling overwhelmed with what he had to do to keep the family and home functioning smoothly. There was a lot of huffing and puffing, which I found quite upsetting. I thought what he had to do was a reasonable amount. I wondered what I was doing to attract this behaviour. I recognized that at a deeper level I was feeling guilty about not doing more. I changed my thoughts to soothe my feelings of unworthiness and laziness, and, within the hour, Bill came to the bedroom to express his love and appreciation of me and to apologize for his grumpiness. He has been in a better mood ever since.

I have realised that, rather than being upset by my children's moods and attitudes I can use them as clues to how I am feeling. If the children are complaining I stop and ask myself how I am feeling. More often than not I realise that I am complaining. If my children are unappreciative I realise that I have probably been unappreciative of them or of myself.

The children's moods are not always reflective of mine. I can tell the difference by how I respond to their mood. If they don't affect me then I wasn't feeling that way but if their negative mood bothers me I can do what I need in order to feel better rather than asking them to change.

As I have used the processes in this book my appreciation for myself has increased dramatically. I realise that I am enough and I do enough for my children. The difference in my children has been phenomenal. Now they are always expressing their appreciation for me and what I do for them. I was looking for appreciation from them because I needed it but now that I don't need it, I get it!

PERSONAL QUALITIES

"Together, let's celebrate what it is to be a mother.
There is no more important work than raising the next generation."
-Alexandra Stoddard

We have looked at the futility of comparing ourselves to others and expecting ourselves to be perfect. Whilst we remember that our value is inherent, that is, we do not have to do anything to deserve self-love, it is worth looking more closely at our unique characteristics and strengths. In your journal, answer the following questions. Take your time.

What do I like about who I am?
What positive characteristics do I have?
What have I achieved in my life? What are my accomplishments?
What are the successes in my life?
What challenges have I overcome?
What are the attributes that I admire in others that I also have?
If someone shared my identical characteristics, what would I admire in them?
How might someone who cared about me describe me?
What do I think my friends like best about me?
What compliments would I give myself?

Remember to include everything, no matter how small, insignificant, modest or unimportant you think it is.

We are not used to singing our praises in our society but we want our children to feel good about themselves and recognise their strengths, so we can set them a good example by celebrating our own strengths. We are not boasting, just recognising the gifts we have.

VALUING OUR ROLE

"Everything I am or ever hope to be... I owe to my angel mother."
-Abraham Lincoln

ADJUSTING TO PARENTHOOD

"A mother can take the place of anyone
But no one can take the place of a mother."
-Cardinal Mermillod

My musings have led me to the conclusion that there are several reasons why being a mum might be proving more difficult than we first expected.

-You realise the enormity of the task. The way you treat your child could affect him or her for the rest of their lives. You want the best for your children. You want them to be happy, but often don't know how to achieve this, leaving you feeling frustrated.

-You will have very little, if any, formal training. You might do antenatal classes learning, for example, or how to bathe or feed a baby.

-You might receive some informal training. Some of us will have seen good examples of mothering from others but this is certainly not guaranteed. You may be trying to emulate a parent you admire but haven't considered that you have your own unique preferences and style. You may have set out with the intention of raising your children in a very different way to the way you were raised, but often we find ourselves repeating the behaviour we received or we react in the opposite way, which might bring its own problems. For example, if you were raised in a strict environment you might now be very lenient.

-The monetary pay is minimal. There is no annual review, no feedback, no encouragement, and no pay rise.

-The role is 24/7. You will have no guaranteed breaks, holidays, or back up.

-You may be isolated for long periods of time. Even if you meet up with other mums you may not feel able to share your concerns with them as motherhood can be quite competitive and judgemental.

-Society in general, although offering you very little support, has great expectations of how you will fulfil you role and is often quick to judge you.

-This job will call on all your emotional reserves. Your whole personality will be involved in the process. All your insecurities will be highlighted and your children will press buttons you didn't know you had.

If that job was advertised in the Job Centre I don't think there would be many takers. I am not highlighting how difficult being a mum is so we can all feel sorry for ourselves, but so we can give ourselves a pat on the back for doing well and take regular breaks that we deserve and need.

WHAT I HAVE ACHIEVED TODAY?

*"What you get by achieving your goals
is not as important as what you become by achieving your goals."*
-Zig Ziglar

We live in a society that values productivity and activity. Often, what we do as a mum goes unnoticed and is grossly undervalued. For example, wiping snotty noses, counselling an upset teenager, or washing the dishes isn't seen as important work. This can lead to us overstretching ourselves, feeling tired with no buffer for unexpected events, and having no time to relax. You have probably heard the saying that *a woman's work is never done.* Also, there is a common expectation that a mum sacrifices her own needs and wants for her child. You can see how all these factors come together so that we don't prioritise our own happiness.

With so much to do and no official breaks it would be all too easy for us to neglect to do what we want to do, and then we can easily become resentful. We feel upset and angry that our children don't appreciate all the little sacrifices we make for them. But maybe we don't have to make sacrifices, at least not as many as we do.

Unless we realise the importance of our happiness when it comes to being the best parent we can be, we could easily neglect to look after ourselves.

Before we spend time considering the balance of our lives let's look in more detail at what we achieve in a day.

Think back over today or yesterday and list all your achievements.

For example:
Got myself and the children washed and dressed
Did some laundry
Prepared meals and washed dishes.

Did some housework

Did some DIY

Paid some bills, organized paperwork and made some necessary telephone calls

Soothed an upset child

Helped with schoolwork

Listened to a child as they considered a decision they wanted to make

Played with my child

Took children to an activity.

Remember, your value is independent of what you do. This exercise is simply to counteract a parent's natural tendency to underestimate what they achieve in a day which might lead to lack of self-appreciation and overwhelment.

FEELING PROUD

"Parenting is the easiest thing in the world to have an opinion about but the hardest thing in the world to do."
-Matt Walsh

In my role as a parenting coach, I had been in the newspaper, on the radio and on television for the first time. I was pleased with this unexpected turn of events. I could now see an easy way of reaching and encouraging more parents. I realised that I could concentrate on writing rather than delivering workshops, at least for the time being, and this fitted around my family perfectly.

A well-meaning friend commented that they were proud of me and, although I recognised the loving sentiment, it highlighted the fact that the role of a parent is often underestimated.

Being on the TV was a breeze compared to the day to day running of a family. Dealing with the emotions of teenagers and toddlers and the sleepless nights caused by a baby had called on all my resources. I had been a parent for 20 years and experienced untold sacrifice and emotional trauma. I had raised and was still in the process of raising confident, independent, loving human beings. Now that is something to be proud of!

Parenting can be a thankless task. I believe it is so important to give ourselves credit for the incredible job we are doing, especially as we probably won't get the appreciation and validation we need from others.

ALL WORK AND NO PLAY

*"Happiness is not a matter of intensity
but of balance, harmony, rhythm and order."*
-Thomas Merton

Positive psychologists tell us that in order to be happy we need to experience three positive emotions for every one negative emotion. One way of experiencing positive emotion is to do things that please us. As parents we often sacrifice our own needs and wants, putting other family members' needs first. So how, in the midst of busy family life, can we find time to do more of what we want?

Consider an activity that you do regularly and ask yourself these questions?

Am I enjoying this?

Do I have to do it?

Can I do it less often or more efficiently?

Can I share the workload by delegating or paying someone to do it?

If I have to do it how can I feel good about it?

It is really worth spending time to do this exercise.

If I absolutely have to do a task I make sure I get in a good mood first. One way is to turn a 'have to' into a 'want to'. For example I might use the chore of cleaning the kitchen as an opportunity to listen to my favourite music or an inspirational speaker. I can focus on the end product of a clean and tidy (or at least cleaner and tidier) kitchen rather than on the initial state of the kitchen. I can be thankful for all the members of the family that have contributed to the mess and appreciate them rather than focus on the work they have created.

Younger children could have their own bowl of water, sitting on a towel to catch the inevitable spills, so that they could 'help'.

Getting in a good mood before attempting a task is always time well spent. Sometimes the best thing to do is nothing. For example, I have a drawer where I keep all my bits and pieces that don't really have a place. Many of you will have a similar drawer where you keep the countless pieces of plastic that don't have a proper home but might be important, bits of string, batteries and keys that don't seemingly open anything but might be needed.

Occasionally this drawer becomes so full that it won't shut fully. If I am in a bad mood I do not attempt to tidy out the drawer. I would throw out the piece of plastic that I subsequently find is an integral part of a child's toy or the key that was useful after all. In my stressed state of mind I wouldn't remember where I had put anything. Also, when I am in a bad mood the task seems larger than when I am in a good mood were I can quickly and efficiently know what to keep and what to throw away.

DO ONLY WHAT YOU WANT TO DO

"When you are what you do,
when you don't, you aren't."
-Dr Wayne Dyer

When we take the time to listen to our inner guidance system and learn that our value is not related to the amount of struggle or sacrifice we undergo, we become free to choose, "What do I want to do?"

We fear that if we only do what we want to do then not much would get done, but I have found that the opposite is the case. Not only do we become more productive and efficient, but we also have fun in the process.

There are many things that you may feel need to be done, and often a simple reframing process could turn the event from a "have to" or "should do" into a "want to." For example, I was sweeping this morning when I heard my thoughts, *I hate doing this every day.* As you can imagine I didn't feel very joyful and I quickly changed my thoughts to, *I like having a clean and tidy home.* I also added, *other members of the family are helping to keep the place orderly and clean.* Another thought that helped was, *the house can't be perfectly clean and tidy all the time. It is natural for it to be messy and dirty at times as we live in it freely.*

At times we do things because we want the approval of others. I have found that if I don't give myself credit for what I do then I look to others to appreciate me. When they don't appreciate me I often feel resentful. So nowadays, rather than doing things to gain others approval and praise I do things for my own pleasure. I still might do the same things I did before but now my motives are different. Ironically when I appreciate myself and therefore don't need others appreciation, that's when I often receive it from others.

As a parent there are so many things we could be doing, and it is easy to feel guilty that we have not given our child every experience available. I remember reading the words of a wise person who said that we have to leave some things for our children to discover for themselves when they leave home. You might find that your child becomes more peaceful and able to entertain themselves more as you slow down your pace of life.

In the past I have ran a Sunday School, Parents and Toddler's group, and a Youth Club, but as my family has grown in size I have learned to say no to requests for help. I have learned to listen to my inner voice that tells me if I am doing something out of a sense of duty or because I will enjoy it. I have found that doing things from a sense of duty doesn't benefit anyone and can be counterproductive. There will always be some cause or group that could do with an extra pair of hands and I understand that volunteering can be a wonderful experience, but I advise you to only do what you feel would enhance your life, not what you think you "should" be doing. Remember, your value is not related to the amount of activities you accomplish in a day. When you take the time to feel good, any action you take will be beneficial to you and others.

The process of writing this book has taught me the importance of not doing something just because I can. On several occasions I have given myself a migraine because I have felt a sense of urgency about completing the book. I have a five-week old baby to care for so have put pressure on myself to write when he is asleep so I can concentrate fully (and have two hands to type with). I have told myself that there is no rush to finish the book. There is no deadline. The book is a joy to write when I wait for the inspiration to "want" to write rather than writing when I feel like I should. I want to write more books when this one is complete so I had better get used to the feeling of a book being unfinished. Like the saying, "A woman's work is never done." There will always be more jobs that could be done each day or more writing that could be done, but I often say to myself, "Enough for today." Or I might even say, "I'm doing no housework or writing today." Sometimes I think I want to write but when I pay closer attention to my feelings I realise that I'm feeling a sense of urgency whereas what I truly want to do is have a hot bath, take a walk, or watch TV.

When we are more realistic about what we can achieve in a day, and spend more time for relaxing we can cope better with unexpected occurrences, for example, the newly dirtied nappy as we are about to leave the house, the spilt milk, the lost shoe. Most of my previous stresses occurred because I didn't have a buffer of time so everything was rushed and I couldn't cope with anything less than compliance from my children. My body was in an adrenaline fuelled state of fight or flight and anger was a common reaction.

Over the next few days try to be aware of negative emotion raised by 'having' to do things.

Do you really have to? If the answer is yes, for example, collecting the children from school, then line up with that decision and realise you want to pick them up rather than leave them there. Maybe there are other options you could consider, for example, joining forces with another parent to share the job of collecting each other's children.

If the answer to the question, "Do I really have to?" is 'No' then consider why you do it and whether you might want to stop doing it. Again, if you decide to do it anyway then line up with it in order to feel good about doing it.

TAKING INSPIRED ACTION

"All the effort in the world won't matter if you are not inspired."
-Chuck Palahniuk

I used to think that I hated shopping. I have realised that I quite enjoy shopping. I just don't like shopping with children in tow. I recently took four of my children to a retail park to buy Christmas presents for their friends. In the past these trips have been arduous to say the least. This time I decided to set a few more ground rules.

A maximum amount was set for each child we were buying for. If one of my children wanted to spend more than the agreed amount it would have to be out of their pocket money. In the past I have huffed and puffed my way around the shop as I negotiated what my children could or could not buy.

I begrudged the money that was spent on presents I didn't think were worth it. This time I made peace with the fact that the children were going to buy things that I might not have chosen. Because of this I could focus on the joy that my children were experiencing as they considered what their friends might like.

My children have a lot of mutual friends so before we left the house we decided who was buying presents for whom. This was not debatable once we were at the shops. I also decided that we would just buy for friends during this shopping trip. We would shop again to buy presents for family members.

On another occasion I really did bite off more than I could chew. We had spent most of the afternoon walking around town, clothes shopping. I had a restless baby and I was hot and bothered. Negative thoughts were swirling around my head until I thought I might scream. Knowing better I decided to take the baby into a changing room to feed and settle. That way I had a few minutes rest and a chance to collect my thoughts. *Everybody is happy with what they*

74

have bought so far. We have almost finished. I can sit quietly while the teenagers help the younger children find the last few items they need. Getting cross isn't going to make the trip end sooner. We can afford the clothes. The staff are helpful. We have transport. One of the children can make me a nice cup of tea when we get home. The weather is warm and dry so no mad dashes to the car to avoid the rain.

On another occasion, my husband was taking the children to a pantomime. I was planning to take the baby to the local town to buy some clothes for him. As the family left the house I realised that what I really wanted to do was take a nap with the baby. Because the shopping trip had been planned for several days it took me a while to realise that I didn't actually have to go there and then. When I checked my diary I learned that it would be more convenient to go later in the week. When I eventually did go shopping with the baby I was full of energy and we had a relaxing and productive day.

DELEGATION IS NOT A DIRTY WORD

"You can do anything, but not everything."
-David Allen

People often ask me how I manage a family of 8 children and the easy answer is I delegate. It took me a long time to learn to delegate. I used to feel guilty asking the children to help with housework. I didn't want to interfere with whatever they were doing, be it educational activities, playing or relaxing. As my family grew I just had to ask for help but I would feel guilty and the children seemed to sense that. They would complain until I either did it myself or lost my temper and forced them to help.

It has taken a lot of practise but nowadays the chores are shared more fairly. I explained to the children that everyone has to contribute in order for the household to run smoothly and to give me time to be able to facilitate their activities. We discussed what household chores each person would like to help with and together we came up with a rota that we modify from time to time as circumstances change. Emily, the eldest daughter at home, helps with laundry as she can fit that around her college work. Alice loves to cook so helps with preparing tea. Elizabeth is still educated at home and can easily help with washing the dishes and keeping the kitchen tidy throughout the day. Grace empties the dishwasher with a little help from her apprentice, Charlotte. John will prepare himself cold food and tidy up after himself. Most days, everyone will get together before or after the evening meal to tidy the house. Every now and again we will spend more time cleaning and tidying the house as a family. Reluctant children are motivated by the promise of a fun activity when the chores are completed. Playing music while we all work together also ensures that the process is as enjoyable as possible. There are times when one of my children might feel that the chores are being distributed unfairly and I take their concern seriously. No one likes to feel they are doing more than their fair share of the workload. The children receive pocket money and they can offer to do a paid job like sweeping the yard or cleaning the cars for extra money.

I almost forgot to mention my hardworking husband. For years I have tried to enrol him into helping with looking after the younger children but he is reluctant. I think he has changed two nappies in his life! As well as working full time Bill is happy to clean windows and cars and enjoys food shopping so I gladly accept his help with that along with other jobs that he does when needed which gives me time to care for the younger children.

Since I stopped feeling guilty about asking the children to help they sensed that complaining was futile and stopped. Now that the workload is shared fairly, not only does the house run smoothly but my children are learning valuable life skills. The research outcomes of a long-term study of eighty-four young adults determined that "the best predictor of young adults' success in their mid-20s was that they participated in household tasks when they were three or four." The researcher, Marty Rossmann, emeritus associate professor of family education at the University of Minnesota, found that by involving the children in tasks parents taught them a sense of responsibility, competence, self-reliance, and self-worth that stayed with them throughout their lives.(Hopgood:pg231)

POSITIVE EMOTIONS

'Enjoy the little things in life,
Because one day you will look back and realise
that they were the big things.'
-Robert Brault

The recommendation from positive psychologists is that we make deliberate efforts to increase the number of times we experience positive emotions. They have found that when we experience a high number of positive emotions, we are more resilient. That is, we are more able to deal with and bounce back from unwanted events and negative emotions.

They have found that rather than one big event making us happy, we need a steady diet of positive emotions to keep us happy. They suggest that we need to experience at least three positive emotions for every negative emotion we experience in order for us to flourish.

Positive psychologists categorize positive emotions into the following ten emotions:

Joy
Gratitude
Serenity
Interest
Hope
Pride
Amusement
Inspiration
Awe
Love (The King or Queen) of Emotions

Working through the list, consider how you might increase the number of times you experience that positive emotion. For example, taking a walk to a local beauty spot might increase your levels of serenity and awe. Contemplating the achievements of yourself or a loved one might increase your feelings of pride. Researching the lives of people who you admire should increase your interest and inspiration. Watching a funny film will increase the amount of humour in your life. Meditation has been shown to increase all of the positive emotions.

What might stop you from doing more of the things you enjoy or taking more breaks this week?

When would be the best time to do something for you?

What might you say to yourself in order to prioritize these activities?

For example,
Life is not all about work. Life is meant to be fun.
My value has nothing to do with what I achieve. For example, I tidy my house because I like a tidy house, not to seek anyone else's approval.
I don't have official breaks so I need to plan my own.
I know better than anyone else what I need to be happy.
My family life is less stressful and more fun if we are not rushing.
I can recognise and deal with negative emotion more easily when I have regular quiet times.
I am a better mum when I have done things that please me.
My children will be okay with someone else looking after them for a while.
I wouldn't want my children to stop living their own lives when they have children.

Positive psychologists is a term describing psychologists who specialize in researching or applying what makes people, organizations or communities thrive.

LOOK AFTER YOURSELF FIRST

*"If people sat outside and looked at the stars each night,
I'll bet they'd live a lot differently."*
-Bill Watterson

It is especially easy as a parent, with a never ending to-do list, to feel the need for continuous activity. In the past, we might have naturally experienced time of quiet reflection while we did laborious jobs or sat quietly sewing or knitting at the end of the day. With so many distractions and pressures on our time it is easy to go through the whole day without a period of quiet.

To get the most out of life and to be the most complete, centred, happy person we can be we need periods of enjoyable activity balanced by periods of contemplation and relaxation. So I encourage you to take as many breaks as possible to reconnect with who you really are. It might be a few seconds deep breathing while waiting at the traffic lights, or longer periods of time sat 'doing nothing,' for example, looking at a beautiful view, stroking your pet, drawing, or listening to uplifting music. I have started meditating after years of putting it off, saying I was too busy. A great analogy I came across is that starting the day without meditating is like walking the ten miles to work because you are too busy to look for your car keys. It is worth making the time for this beneficial practice. I feel calmer, more focused, and more joyful as I notice more of life's blessings and I can notice and deal with negative thoughts far more easily. Often, I decide to take the day off to remember my inherent value. I always end the day feeling awesome and I am much more productive than my previous scattered efforts.

You have probably heard of the analogy of someone on an aeroplane that is about to make an emergency landing. They need to put their own oxygen mask on before they put a mask on their child. If the parent collapses due to lack of oxygen they are no help to their child. Being selfish is not a dirty word.

Aiming for harmony and rhythm by listening to my inner guidance has helped me to move through my day in a more pleasing way. For example, I love to write and am tempted to write many times throughout the day even though I am only able to write a few times a week. On one occasion I had returned from a walk with the baby who was asleep. This seemed like a perfect opportunity to write but I recognised that, in this moment, my desire to write was due to a sense of urgency rather than pleasure. My work was to soothe this sense of urgency rather than to write.

I realised that what I really wanted to do was visit the gym. Everyone in the house was happy and didn't want to come with me so I decided to go for a swim on my own. I would be back within the hour. I am so glad because sitting in the steam room listening to Frankie Goes To Hollywood's *The Power Of Love* was not to be missed.

ENJOY THE JOURNEY

"A happy life is just a string of happy moments.
Most people don't allow the happy moment because they're so busy
trying to get a happy life."
-Abraham Hicks

Often, we miss out on the joy of the everyday as we contemplate all the things we could be doing that we think would make us happy.

It is January right now, the time when people in the UK typically book their summer holidays. The media is full of advertisements and two TV adverts have stood out to me. One advert tells the story of a family of bears. Sad music is playing as we see Dad Bear squashed on public transport as he makes his daily commute to work. Mum Bear is at work looking mournfully at a picture on her desk of her children. Two younger bears are observed eating TV dinners or listening to music through their headphones, oblivious to the people around them. Dad Bear has missed the chance to connect with his children as he arrives home after their bedtime. The mood changes as the family drive to a holiday park. They have fun and the family members reconnect with each other.

The second advert has a similar theme and follows the woes of a little girl's teddy bear as he is treated neglectfully on a daily basis. He then goes on holiday with the little girl and her family and life is wonderful again.

How many of us live our lives like this? We get through each day, either at home or at work. We count the days until the weekend or the holidays. Perhaps we dream of winning the lottery so we can leave our jobs or the daily grind. We might be looking forward to the time when the children leave home so we will finally have a clean and tidy home and more free time.

When I talk to older parents whose children have left the nest they tell me that the days when their children were at home were the best days of their lives. So the question is, "How can we make our everyday lives more like a holiday?"

I was at a nature reserve the other day with the children when we decided to take a walk to the lake. The path doubled back on itself and I thought to myself, *The path could have gone straight to the lake rather than take this winding route.* Then it struck me that this is how I approach life, always thinking about the destination rather than enjoying the journey. Of course the path could have been a lot shorter but what would be the point of that? I was passing beautiful flowers, picking blackberries, feeling the sun on my skin, watching the children laughing and running ahead of me, and enjoying this adventure.

I read a book a year or so ago entitled, *The Power of Now,* by a German guy named Eckhart Tolle. When he was a youngster he received a scholarship for a place at Oxford University. He had a good reason to be happy yet he was in the pit of despair. He recalls saying, "I cannot live with myself any longer." This got him to thinking who is this "I" and who is this "myself?" After some more thought he concluded that the "I" was the deep pure unspoiled essence of himself and the "myself" was all the things he had been telling himself was true for years, things he had learnt were true, which he was now realising weren't necessarily true. He had lots of 'shoulds' and 'oughts' about himself.

He then decided to spend some time getting to know his true self. One conclusion he came to was that people tend to rush around from one activity or experience to the next trying to fill a void, trying to find that thing that will make them happy, never living in the moment but always thinking, "What's next? Maybe that moment will be better than this one?" He decided that living meant totally experiencing each moment as it presents itself. You might have heard the saying, "yesterday is history, tomorrow is a mystery, today is a gift from God, that's why it's called the present."

When we slow down we will be in a better position to recognise our feelings and the thoughts behind them.

By slowing down and journaling about how I feel, I sometimes feel strong negative emotions come to the surface. These feelings might have been buried by years of keeping too busy to notice them or address them properly. When these strong negative emotions become apparent we can show ourselves unconditional love. We can talk to ourselves the way we imagine a wonderfully loving friend might.

What things could you do this week that would give you an opportunity to be quiet and be more aware of your thoughts? Every day this week choose to do at least one thing for you and you alone. For example, take a leisurely bath, listen to your choice of music (instead of nursery rhymes), take a walk, do some exercise, go for a swim, have a lie in. Consider starting the day with meditation, and so on.

Happiness is a journey, not a destination.

"You will never have this day with your children again.
Tomorrow they will be a little older than they were today.
This day is a gift.
Just breathe, notice, delight in their faces, hands and feet.
Pay attention.
Relish the charms of the present.
Enjoy today.
It will be over before you know it."

SPINNING PLATES

"The key is not to prioritize what's on your schedule,
but to schedule your priorities."
Stephen Covey

I was recently interviewed for a TV channel specializing in relationship advice. The topic was, *Who should be prioritized in the family?* My premise is that a mum has to look after herself well in order to look after her family. When asked the question of who should be prioritized I almost said *me* but that wouldn't have been the whole story.

As a mum I will want to enable my children to get their needs and wants met. I will sometimes put my desires on hold in order to facilitate their wishes. If I have a partner I will want to consider their needs as well.

After further consideration, I answered that the family is like a team and works best if very member of the team is at their best and playing to their strengths. When it feels difficult to enable everyone to get what they want I try to stay upbeat, trusting that a solution can be found.

A recent example involved a walk through the woods to a local pub for lunch. My husband had initiated this ritual as a way of spending time together in a way that we would both be happy as I love to walk and he loves pub lunches. I was feeling uncomfortable at leaving the children on this occasion as we had been away from them the day before and would be going out the day after without them. I felt torn between my husband and the children. I wanted us to take the children to the park but Bill was not happy. Previously I would have been bad tempered with my husband, accusing him of being selfish. This time I tried to understand Bill's point of view and be solution focused. We decided to take the children with us to the pub. Although the walk was a little longer than they would have liked, the promise of a nice meal at the end kept them motivated. Everyone was happy.

I often feel like a plate spinner. I see each of the children and my husband as a plate and I am continually scanning my plates to see which one is in need of a little extra spin to keep it from toppling from its pole. I recognise that I need to look after myself to do this job well.

The plate spinning analogy has helped me come to terms with the feeling of not wanting any more children after William. This was a new feeling for me so came as a surprise. I now see that I have reached the limit of how many plates I can comfortably spin.

This analogy also helps me to keep balance in my life. I imagine plates to represent categories such as housework, paperwork, decluttering, writing, relaxation. I recognise when a category is requiring more attention and rather than ignoring a task until it is really aggravating me, I give my attention to it and metaphorically give the wobbly plate a little spin.

JUST A MUM

*"The mother is the most precious possession of the nation,
so precious that society advances its highest wellbeing
when it protects the functions of the mother."*
-Ellen Key

"I'm just a mum." How many of us have said that? It's a loaded statement if ever I've heard one. There is no more important role than being a parent and yet our contribution is often undervalued by others and even by ourselves. Often we feel unprepared, inadequate, and overwhelmed. These feelings have an impact on our relationship with our children. An incident that happened yesterday highlighted this to me.

My husband was due to return to work after four weeks of paternity leave. I had greatly appreciated having him at home. The thought of him going back to work and leaving me to organise all the household chores, including those he had been doing, was obviously playing on my mind because I had a mini meltdown. I was still up in the night feeding the baby so I was tired after being out all afternoon with the children. As soon as we arrived home I had to complete the evening meal (my seventeen year old had prepared it earlier) while the other children were doing small chores around the house. One of my daughters was complaining she had more to do than her sibling. If I had been in a good mood I could have easily dealt with this but feeling tired and anxious about my husband's impending return to work meant I lost my temper and I started complaining that no one appreciated all the work I did.

In the past this could have blown into an anger outburst of epic proportions resulting in most of the family feeling upset and angry. Now that I knew that life is supposed to feel good to us and that my feelings are my guidance system, I was able to choose a different course of action. If I feel bad the best course of action is to find a way to feel good again before I do or say anything else, so I took myself off and spent ten minutes finding better feeling thoughts. I showed myself compassion by realising I was tired and could look forward to an early night. I showed my children compassion by recognising that it is perfectly acceptable to want the workload to be shared fairly.

It also made me realise that I wasn't valuing my role as a housewife and mum and that is why I was looking for appreciation from others. I didn't want to rely on anyone else's approval so I reassured myself that I was doing a great job.

Feeling better, I went to find my daughter whom I found playing happily, so no harm was done.

DECISIONS, DECISIONS

"Never regret. If it's good, it's wonderful,
if it's bad, it's experience."
-Victoria Holt

Being a parent involves making a lot of decisions. Often we have more freedom of choice and flexibility than if we were working for someone else. We are our own boss. Because there are no definitive rules regarding parenting, we often look to society, our extended family or our peer group for guidance on how to be a parent.

As children, we were probably brought up to do what others told us. Parents and teachers expected certain behaviours from us. We might have complied even when we didn't really want to do what was being asked because it was the easiest thing to do at the time. Maybe we didn't cooperate as our desire to make our own decisions was so strong it was worth facing the consequences of disobedience. Our days may have been mapped out for us and we may have unquestioningly followed what others thought we should do with our lives.

As a student, and then an employee, I liked not having to decide what to do moment by moment, and I liked to receive regular feedback on my performance. As a young parent I looked around me for guidance on how to be a mum. In the early days of motherhood I was a Christian and looked to the Bible and Christian friends for instruction and guidance. Over the years I have been increasingly drawn to a way of parenting that respects my child's autonomy (their right to make their own decisions) but my own insecurities and need to have my children behave in a certain way in order for me to feel happy still caused lots of problems.

Now I am learning to use my own guidance system. Some call this their inner being or their gut instinct. When we are sensitive to how we feel when we make a decision we can guide ourselves. I believe that each family is unique and that is why I don't offer specific advice on topics such as using dummies, bedtimes, mealtimes, and so on.

When I am making a decision I ask myself, "What do *I* want to do?" I ask myself if my decision is being made only to please other people or because I think I should be doing a particular thing.

LINE UP WITH DECISIONS

*"You don't have to defend or explain your decisions to anyone.
It's your life. Live without apologies."*
-Mandy Hale

In the past I have found decision making difficult because I wanted things to be black and white, a definite yes or no, this way or that way. Now I think of a see saw or balance when I have a choice to make. I ask myself which way is the balance tipping and then make that my choice.

Following this, I find it beneficial to think thoughts that support that decision rather than thinking how things might have been if we had made a different decision. Easier said, we "line up" with the decision. There are no wrong decisions. A decision will either turn out the way we wanted it to or it will be a learning experience. When a decision we take leads us into a situation we don't like we can make a new decision. Regretting a decision we make leads to us feeling bad, keeping us in the unwanted place for longer. The best thing we can do in that instance is to be kind to ourselves, reminding ourselves that we made the best decision we could at the time. If contrast comes from the decision we know that contrast can lead to growth when we accept it.

One morning I was lying in bed wondering whether to get up or stay in bed. I had been up feeding and changing the baby and he had gone back to sleep. The rest of the family were still asleep so I could have easily stayed in bed or I could have got up to do a few chores. This might not sound like a big decision but in the past I could have easily let this decision put me in a bad mood by focusing on all the negative consequences of whatever decision I made. If I had decided to get up but felt tired later I would have berated myself for not taking the opportunity to have a lie in. If I stayed in bed I might have felt grumpy later if I felt that I had too many chores to do in too little time. Instead, I decided to line up with whatever decision I made.

If I get up: I can catch a nap later in the day. I can shower and dress while the baby is asleep, not needing my attention. I might be able to get some chores or even some writing done.

If I stay in bed: I will enjoy the comfort of my bed and feel more rested. I can take a shower later when the older children are around to keep an eye on the baby. I have all day to do my jobs. I have plenty of time to do what I want to do so there is no rush to get up.

'SHOULD' IS NOT A GOOD ENOUGH REASON

"Just because you can doesn't mean you should."
-Sherrilyn Kenyon

When I asked my parenting friends what their main negative emotion was, the outstanding response was 'guilt'. We constantly feel that we have done enough for our children. So I was not alone.

We had enjoyed a lovely Christmas break. My daughter had been home from university and my husband, a teacher, had been off for the school holidays. I had enjoyed the time we had spent together as a family. We had fun chatting, eating, visiting with friends, going for walks, swimming at the local pool, watching movies, playing with new presents. The holidays were coming to an end. My daughter had returned to university the day before and my husband was due to return to work in a couple of days. It was time for the Christmas decorations to come down and I was feeling melancholy.

I was chatting with Bill, trying to work out why I was in a low mood. It wasn't just because the holidays were coming to an end as we had lots of fun things planned over the following few weeks. I realised I was feeling anxious that we hadn't done more with the children over the holidays and the opportunity to do things as a family was coming to an end, at least until the next school holidays.

Bill reminded me that I often have this feeling. If the children haven't been out for a few days I start worrying that I should be doing more for them. In fact, the children were quite happy and weren't asking to go anywhere. My anxiety was caused by thinking that I 'should' be taking the children out if I could.

I decided to rest and ponder and enjoy the quiet. Bill had taken my seven year old with him to watch a football match, everyone else was entertaining themselves and I was napping and playing with the baby. I was in the middle of reading *How Eskimos Keep Their Babies Warm* by Mei-Ling Hopwood. The book was reminding me that many things I had been told were an absolute truth were in fact just cultural norms. For example, we are told that parents should play with their children for a certain amount of time each day in order to build a close relationship and to help their child's development. In other cultures parents were not involved in their child's play at all. That was left to other children in the community. Mei-Ling investigated various parenting styles across the globe and came to the conclusion that there were many ways to raise a happy child. Parenting issues she investigated included children's bedtimes, healthy eating, the use of pushchairs or slings, potty training, father's involvement, parents playing with their children, discipline and children working.

Even in the United Kingdom cultural norms are constantly changing. Breast feeding, sling wearing, bed sharing are back in fashion but these don't suit everyone. Many parents keep their children busy with the multitude of activities on offer while others choose a more unstructured approach to their child's play. Although we choose to home educate I can see how many children thrive in a school environment. I have always felt that families should be encouraged to find their own preferred approach and not be judged for choosing an approach that isn't considered preferable by society at the time.

A clue that we are following a cultural norm rather than what would suit our own needs and wants is use of the word *should*. If I hear myself saying *should* I stop and question my logic. Who says? How do they know? How do I know? How is this in the best interest of me and my child? Could we try another way to enable everyone to meet their needs?

Be sensitive to any *should* you use as you move through your daily routine with your family.

NO REGRETS

"No regrets, just lessons learned."
-Author unknown

Recently, I spent most of the day in bed nursing a migraine. When I eventually felt well enough to get up everyone was busy doing their own thing, so I decided to write. I had been sat at my desk for about an hour when I looked out of the window and noticed an astonishing sunset. The sky was pink and filled with candyfloss clouds. I looked at my four year old Charlotte, who was skipping happily around the room. For a moment I felt guilty, thinking maybe I should have been playing with her rather than writing but realised that she was happy. I made a quick decision to take Charlotte and the new baby out for a walk. By the time we left the house the sun was almost gone. No more pink sky. We enjoyed the walk anyway. It was good to feel and smell the fresh air. I quietened down my thoughts of, "I should have left earlier."

Did you notice two *shoulds* in the previous paragraph? If I hear myself say *should* it is normally an indication that I am making a decision from a place of guilt rather than from joy. I did what I wanted to do, which resulted in a lovely walk with two of my children.

Later that evening I decided to look at a parenting book. I agreed with much of what the author had to say but one section caused feelings of guilt to resurface. The author was encouraging parents to slow down and savour the time they had with their children. Although I agreed with the sentiment and understood that the author's motive was to encourage I still felt a sense of guilt and regret. I felt guilt that I had not done the best for my child and regret that I had missed opportunities to connect with my child. Rather than focusing on all the opportunities, experiences, and positive attention I had given my children I felt bad for any missed opportunities.

In order to soothe myself into feeling better I remembered several things. My children and I have a lot of good times together. It is natural for everyone to have times when they pursue their own interests, including me. The children don't need me to be available all the time. I stop what I am doing if the children need my attention. I am not my children's only source of joy or help. I enjoy writing and I am learning so much to help me become a better parent.

As a parent there are so many things we could be doing, and it is easy to feel guilty that we have not given our child every experience available especially with pressure from the media to do just that. I remember reading the words of a wise person who said that we have to leave some things for our children to discover for themselves when they leave home. You might find that your child becomes more peaceful and able to entertain themselves more as you slow down your pace of life.

LOVING OUR CHILDREN

"Loving our children is the greatest investment
we can make in this world.
Nothing matters more."
-Author Unknown

HOW I THINK ABOUT MY CHILDREN IS IMPORTANT

"Love your neighbour as you love yourself."
-Holy Bible

The reason I have emphasised self-care and compassion before turning our attention to our children is because I have discovered I cannot give to my children more than I give to myself. To put it simply, we can only love our children as much as we love ourselves.

So how do we love our children in the same way we show love to ourselves? We show them compassion. For example, we realise they are doing their best. We recognise that even at our age we experience and express negative emotion. We give them the benefit of the doubt. We try to see things from their point of view. We recognise that they are not winding us up on purpose. We remember that it matters to them even if it does not seem important to us.

I am not encouraging us to always give in to our child's demands. We want our children to learn to be happy even when things aren't exactly the way they want them to be. We don't want to teach them that complaining always gets them what they want. But we teach with love and gentleness and an eye on their long term development rather than our short-term peace and quiet.

It is human nature to focus on what's wrong. We focus on the one thing that is not how we would like it and pay no or little attention to the ninety-nine things that are working well. The same goes for the way we often judge ourselves and those around us. We fixate on what needs improving rather than dwell on what is working well.

As a parent, we often think it is our job to constantly correct our children so they can lead the best life possible. We think that by pointing out their faults they will be able to eliminate them. Instead, what often happens is that the child feels discouraged and inadequate. What I have learned is that by focusing on our children's strengths and paying as little attention as possible to their areas for

98

growth, we encourage them to be their best selves. When we focus on the positive we will bring out more of that in our child.

Recall some common statements you make about your child(ren). What better feeling thoughts could you make?

Think of one of your children and a particular attitude or behaviour that is bothering you. Can you turn that into a positive?

Make a list of positive aspects of each of your children. Repeat often.

CHILDREN CAN VALUE THEMSELVES

"As you care less about what others think of you,
you will care more about what others think of themselves."
-Stephen Covey

Up until the incident I am about to describe, my eleven year old Elizabeth was the child I clashed with the most. One morning she wanted to ask me a question about whether we could get a dog. It wasn't the first time she had asked! I was working at the computer and wasn't focusing on what she was saying. She shouted at me that I was the worst mum ever and never listened, and then she ran into the bathroom.

I ran after her feeling furious. I hadn't felt such a rage for a long time. I banged on the bathroom door shouting, "How dare you when my whole life revolves around you?"

When the situation had calmed down I had time to reflect and these are the things I concluded:

My whole life did revolve around pleasing them. I had buried so many of my own desires to try to satisfy theirs. No wonder I felt resentful when they didn't appreciate me.

I did feel like I was a terrible mother at times. When they weren't happy I would take it personally, as though I should be able to make them happy.

Maybe I had trained Elizabeth to look to me for her self-esteem by always trying to be available for her. The time I wasn't available to soothe her because I was distracted, left her feeling unsupported.

Because I am an imperfect human I was the wrong focus for her. She needed to look inside for her sense of worth rather than to me. The times when she was the object of my attention and I was feeling other emotions, such as disappointment or anger, must have been difficult for her.

Her outburst (and mine) made me realise that I was hooking my self-worth on to my abilities as a mother. When Elizabeth complained it made me realise that I did feel less than worthy. That is why I reacted so strongly.

So where did we go from there?

I decided to stop looking to my children to value and appreciate me, but rather look to my inner being where I would feel my inherent value.

How many times have we said or heard ourselves or other parents saying, "You don't appreciate what I do for you." I still do things for Elizabeth now, but only if I can do them happily. Sometimes this means saying no to her request. Sometimes I will do what she asks but at a time that suits me better. Sometimes I will help Elizabeth to meet her needs but after some brainstorming we realise we can do it a different way than her original request.

If Elizabeth is feeling negative emotion I suggest she looks at ways of helping herself to feel better before we look at the details of fulfilling the request. Often the request disappears as she soothes herself back into a better mood. Like many of us, Elizabeth believes that changing her circumstances will make her feel better so I have been encouraging her to find ways of changing her outlook. When Elizabeth is feeling negative she often complains to me about what she doesn't want but she isn't able or willing to rephrase her concern into what she does want. She is learning the importance of considering what she does want in helping her to move toward her desire. While she is still at the complaining stage we can't have a constructive conversation so I don't engage with her on that topic until she is prepared to look for solutions and be optimistic.

When Elizabeth is feeling bad I remind her that she has more power than she has been using to make herself happy. She would often blame me for her bad mood but she is learning to look for solutions rather than focus on problems and blaming. For example, if she thinks that not having to share a room with her sister would make her happy but I cannot accommodate that then she is angry at me. She is learning that any feelings of lack of self-worth or lack of appreciation can be remedied internally.

Since the outburst, we have discovered that Elizabeth didn't like herself much at times and was taking her feelings of low self-esteem out on me. We had started a vicious cycle. She felt bad, and behaved in a grumpy and blaming manner, and I reacted in a less than loving way. Subsequently, because she was looking to me for her self-esteem she would continue to feel bad. I wanted to stop the cycle. This leads to the next chapter...

FOCUS ON THE POSITIVE – ELIZABETH

"Love believes the best of others."
-Holy Bible

The incident with Elizabeth happened during a period where we seemed to be clashing a lot. She would be sullen and I would be angry. On a few occasions she said that she didn't think I loved her. I tried to reassure her that I did but her behaviour made it difficult for me to show her. How many parents have been in this situation? We have children and we are full of love for them yet when they behave in a way we don't find pleasing we react in an unpleasant way.

I realised that I was not loving her unconditionally. Her bad mood upset me because it made me feel inadequate as a mum. I needed her to be happy in order to be happy myself. I needed to be reassured that I was doing a good job.

As I recognised my feelings of inadequacy and lack of self-worth, I realised that it wasn't Elizabeth's behaviour that needed to change, but my thoughts of not being enough. I soothed myself with thoughts such as, *I am doing my best. It isn't my job to make Elizabeth happy as she has the power to make herself happy. As I love and forgive myself I will be more able to love Elizabeth unconditionally.*

We then had a meaningful conversation about where her feelings of self-worth and self-love could come from. We discussed our relationship and how we could be individually responsible for our own happiness. We could enjoy each other's company when we were feeling good, and when we felt negative emotion we could look for other ways to soothe ourselves that didn't involve needing each other's positive attention.

My habit had been to focus on Elizabeth's grumpiness and I had lost sight of her positive qualities. I decided to spend some time focusing on her positive qualities.

She is strong minded. I had to encourage one of my other children to not give in so easily to others, but here was a child who knew what she wanted to do and she was not easily persuaded. I had previously seen this as a weakness or at least as an inconvenience to me.

She is witty, and she has a great sense of humour, which has made her very popular. Most nights I hear her and her sister, whom she shares a room with, laughing themselves to sleep.

She is intelligent and can give a reasoned argument. Again, I had previously seen this as a weakness when I wanted her to be compliant so I could be happy.

She is very caring. When she is feeling happy Elizabeth is loving and affectionate with her parents, siblings, and friends. She is thoughtful and gentle.

In conclusion, her behaviour prompted me to recognise that my perception of my self-worth was less than it should have been. This led me to love myself unconditionally, which enabled me to love her unconditionally.

FOCUS ON THE POSITIVE - EMILY

"The secret of change is to focus all of your energy,
not on fighting the old, but on building the new."
-Socrates

It is so tempting to focus on the behaviour of a child who is bringing out negative reactions in us. Instead, we serve ourselves extremely well if we focus on the positive qualities of our children.

A recent episode with my seventeen year old daughter highlights this. She is a free spirit and not a people pleaser, and when she is in a good mood she is fun to be around. She is normally light hearted but recently she has been less than happy because she is going through some learning experiences and trying to work things out. Deadlines at college, a new boyfriend, lack of money, lack of time to earn money (according to her). For several evenings I complained about her to my husband. He patiently listened but we knew there was nothing we could do to force her to improve her attitude. It took me a while to remember the principle that I am in charge of my own happiness and I can't rely on anyone else's good mood to keep me happy. Although it was difficult to do as I wanted to justify my anger my pointing out all the things she was doing 'wrong' I decided to swallow my pride and spend some time considering all of her qualities. As I was doing this I had the insight that she has always been aloof and takes things for granted, but I normally didn't mind because we were getting on well. However, her bad mood made her aloofness unacceptable to me. I felt like I was being used because our close relationship didn't seem to be there. It felt like I wasn't getting anything back from her in exchange for my practical and emotional support of her. The following morning we had a lovely chat and I felt like I had my daughter back. Only the night before I had been thinking how much easier things would be when she left home!

The moral of the story is:

When we focus on what's right, that quality increases to match our expectations.

When we focus on what's wrong, that quality increases to match our expectations.

Or put another way:

Don't try to change other people's behaviour so I can be happy

Be happy so that other people's behaviour will change, and even if it doesn't we can still be happy and love them unconditionally.

If we attempt to manipulate our children they will know it and we won't be able to keep up the pretence of Unconditional Love for long. We genuinely desire to love and accept them for who they are now.

Consider a member of your family who is driving you crazy at the moment. Spend a few minutes listing their positive aspects. Characteristics that annoy you at the moment can be looked at differently to see the positive aspects.

NOTHING IS MORE IMPORTANT THAN ME FEELING GOOD

"Those who are at war with others are not at peace with themselves."
-William Hazlitt

My fourteen year old daughter Alice was upset the other evening. She and her friend had had a disagreement and Alice felt misunderstood. If there is one thing Alice doesn't like it is being thought badly of. Her friend has a new boyfriend and Alice had asked her not to spend too much time with him at an upcoming party as she worried that she would be bored and feel like a third wheel. Her friend had taken the request as a demand and felt insulted that Alice thought she would be so insensitive. Despite a quite in depth email conversation they couldn't seem to see the others' point of view. It was at this point that Alice came to me for help. I felt sad seeing my daughter so upset. What made matters worse was that I was the one who had advised her to mention her concerns to her friend in the first place.

Alice and I had been in this place on many occasions before. Alice is a beautiful and talented person in so many ways but she does tend to see her glass as half empty. Her sensitivity and pessimism had irritated me in the past because I didn't know how to help. Her negativity was resonating with negative aspects of my personality that I hadn't learned how to deal with.

I caught myself beginning to feel bad. I realised that I had been wrong to advise her to speak with her friend but instead she could have considered how to make herself feel better no matter what happened at the party. I was trying to control external circumstances for her rather than teach her that she had control over her thoughts and feelings.

Rather than going down the familiar path of self-blame and upset for Alice I started to wear down a new path of positive thoughts. Remembering that any negative emotion is just an indication of my unhelpful thoughts, kept me from going down a familiar negative thought route.

I showed myself compassion, remembering that I was only just learning myself the importance and power of controlling my own thoughts rather than trying to control external circumstances.

I told myself that we could work this out, it was no big deal, and that nothing had gone wrong. I realised that I was more like Alice than I thought in that I often 'catastrophised' events.

I was tempted to blame Alice's friend for not agreeing to Alice's request and for 'causing' Alice's upset, however I know she had her own unique perspective and she had done nothing wrong either. It was fine; Alice and I didn't need anyone to behave in a certain way for us to feel good.

I explained to Alice that she was upset because her opinion of herself in that moment was self-critical. If she was upset at her friend, then she was being unnecessarily critical of her friend. If Alice thought this was a big deal then, again, she was thinking unhelpful thoughts. All she and I had to do was to find thoughts that would help us to feel better.

These new thoughts included: *It's no big deal, it will blow over in no time; us finding better feeling thoughts will probably help the issue to be resolved; we are loved and acceptable and learning; everyone is loved and accepted and learning; we have control over how we feel and we want to feel good; we do not need to control other people or circumstances in order to feel happy.*

We both felt better immediately and needless to say the 'problem' vanished.

Alice's pessimism irritated me because it was highlighting my own pessimism that I didn't know how to deal with. This fitted with the theory that people are like a mirror, reflecting back to us our strengths and weaknesses. How many times have we heard someone angrily state that they don't like another person because of their temper? Maybe we can remember a time when we gossiped about another person's habit of gossiping. I am becoming more appreciative of all the people who come into my life, even those who I might have otherwise disliked, remembering that they are only highlighting elements in my own personality which I might have been denying. After an encounter with such a person we can consider what character quality we would like and focus on cultivating that in order to become even happier.

FORGIVE AND FORGET

"Forgiveness is the greatest gift you can give yourself."
-Maya Angelou

When we experience something unwanted we often look for someone to blame. If we blame ourselves we will feel guilty, or even depressed if we think these type of thoughts often enough. If we blame the other person in the scenario, either our child or partner, we might feel angry. If we have found the other to be at fault we might try to do something to change them as we think they need to be a certain way in order for us to be happy.

We have already discussed the futility of this approach. Instead, our work is to find better feeling thoughts about ourselves and about the other person.

I was talking to a young mum recently who explained to me that the most difficult thing for her was calming down after she had lost her temper with her young son.

After a brief conversation she began to see what the problem was. In order to justify her angry outburst she was focusing on her son's "misbehaviour," which was keeping her angry feelings stirred up. She had the false belief that someone had to be at fault and it was too painful to think it might be her. Her self-esteem couldn't take another bashing!

The solution she happily discovered was that no one needed to take the blame.

Once she recognised the pattern she had created, she could learn to talk to herself kindly. This self-compassion then gave her the strength and insight to show compassion to her son.

Arguments can be forgiven and forgotten much easier now.

WATCH YOUR LANGUAGE

*"Words have the power to build up,
or the power to tear down."*
-The Holy Bible

The words we use to communicate with or about our children are very influential.

Have you ever been asked, "Is your baby good?" We all know that the intention of the person asking is friendly but think about what the question implies. If the answer is no, then does this mean the baby is bad? A better question would be, "Is the baby content?" An even better question would be, "How are you?" Even better still, "Is there anything I can do to help you in this enormously valuable role of raising the next generation?"

If the child is compliant, easy going, content, and therefore giving us an easy time then they are considered good. If they are unsettled, needing a lot of attention, not needing a lot of sleep or in pain then they are considered to be not good. Our definition of them depends on how they impact us. Of course, we are all good; it's just that some children are easier to parent than others.

I believe that we continue this theme as the child grows.

Considering the language we use when we refer to our children might help us to see them in a more positive light, and therefore improve our feelings towards them.

For example, we might complain that our child is strong willed because they don't comply with us, but would we want them to be weak willed? We might refer to our precious daughter as a 'little madam' when we could say that they are learning how to be unconditionally happy (as we all are). A child could be seen as determined rather than stubborn. A fussy child knows what they like and what they don't.

Taking the time to consider the world through the child's eyes will help us enormously. We start to consider what it is they need and want rather than how their behaviour is affecting or inconveniencing us.

LOVE LANGUAGES

"Sometimes you love people in a language they cannot understand."
-Gary Chapman

Gary Chapman, director of Marriage and Family Life Consultants, Inc. has written a series of books exploring a concept he calls, "The Five Love Languages." In his books Gary explores the idea that each person has a preferred love language. The five languages he describes are: Words of affirmation; Quality time; Receiving gifts; Acts of service; Physical touch. His theory is that relationship difficulties can often be resolved by recognising the love language of yourself and those you love and 'speaking' in that language to each other. For example, if my language is acts of service, that is I show my love to my partner or child, by doing things for him or her, but if their language is quality time then my love might not be recognised by them if I cook for them, but don't make time to sit and chat with them. Gifts might be wasted on a person whose primary love language is words of affirmation, that is, they like to hear your appreciation of them verbally rather than with a gift.

I have used Gary's concepts of love languages with my children. My primary love language is quality time so I thought my children would know my love for them by my presence. I have found that learning and 'speaking' my individual child's language has made our relationship much healthier and it has prevented miscommunication. For example, my least favoured love language is gifts, so I have learned to put my natural inclinations of not spending money on things I deem frivolous aside in order to show love to my children whose primary love language is gifts. I am learning to consider all the love languages when I want to express my love to each of my children.

While we desire that our children become reliant on their own inner being for their source of self-esteem, it is nice to show them the love we feel for them in a way that they can easily hear and understand.

For example:

Words of Affirmation; Choosing words carefully. Asking ourselves whether we are in a good mood before we speak. I have to be careful what I say about my children to others, especially when my children are around. It might seem like harmless chat to me but could offend my child unknowingly.

Quality Time; Sitting together without distractions and listening to whatever is on their mind. This could be anything from problems with relationships at school or discussion about the characters of their favourite TV show (I have to remember that even though the TV show is uninteresting to me, it is interesting to them).

Receiving Gifts; Gifts is my least favoured love language but, with some of my children, a little gift goes a long way in showing my love for them.

Acts of Service; Of course this will depend on the child's age but just making my child a cup of tea while they are studying is an easy way to show them love.

Physical Touch; Giving my children hugs and kisses comes easily when I am feeling loved but physical touch is the love language I find most difficult when I am not happy.

This leads me to my next point, which is, in order to show love to our children it is important that we are feeling loved ourselves. I have realised that we can use the concept of love languages to show love to ourselves.

For example:

Words of Affirmation; Be aware of how you speak to yourself. I use my journal to write out positive words of affirmation reminding myself that I am doing a good job and I am valuable.

Quality Time; Spending time just being rather than doing. Taking a walk or a leisurely bath is a way of showing love to yourself.

Receiving Gifts; You don't need to blow the budget in order to treat yourself to some new clothes or a nice meal.

Acts of Service; Can you pay someone to do a job that you don't enjoy? This will leave you with more free time to do the things you do enjoy. Ask for the help you need and deserve.

Physical Touch. Don't be afraid to ask for a hug. Or why not treat yourself to a massage or a facial?

Consider what your primary love language is and come up with as many ways as you can to show love to yourself.

Consider the preferred love language of each of your children and come up with as many ways as you can to show love to them.

DON'T WORRY, BE HAPPY

*"There are two gifts we should give our children,
one is roots and the other is wings."*
-Hodding Carter

I remember hearing a radio conversation several years ago about so-called 'hover parenting' parents who were over-protective to the point where children are not given the room to make their own decisions and learn from their mistakes. My eldest daughter was fifteen at the time and I realised that I was, indeed, a hover parent.

Like many parents, I was constantly checking if my daughter had done what I considered enough studying for her to pass her exams. I used to say that 'we' were doing GCSEs. Of course, she was the one doing the GCSEs but I was so involved emotionally that I felt I was doing them as well. I had told myself that once the exams were over I would be able to stop worrying.

It became clear to me that there would always be something to worry about. I realised that as soon as one 'problem' I had been worrying about had passed, I would immediately begin focusing on another problem. There would be further studies, relationships, employment, money, homes, and mortgages. I didn't want to spend the rest of my life worrying about my children, and I had seven more children to worry about after Rachel.

That day I decided I would have to stop worrying about my children.

Now when my children come to me with various issues I don't feel weighed down but stay emotionally strong, using the processes in this book, so I can help them gain a hopeful perspective on whatever is bothering them.

On the subject of teenagers, I recently heard a comment that if we want our children to stay off drugs and excessive alcohol use then the best thing we can do is to show them that we can be happy without these things. If they see us not taking drugs or excessive alcohol but they see us miserable then they might be tempted to ignore our advice because they don't want to be miserable themselves.

As we learn to be more unconditionally happy, valuing ourselves and others and appreciating our lives, we set our children the best example possible. It is unlikely that they will take all of our advice as they have their own lessons to learn and their own unique desires but at least we will have some credibility in their eyes if we are mostly happy. As they witness us dealing with negative emotion they learn valuable skills to help them deal with their own, inevitable, negative emotion.

CHILDREN MAKE THEIR OWN DECISIONS

"Children learn how to make good decisions by making decisions,
not by following directions."
-Alfie Kohn

When making decisions which affect our children it is a good idea to ask ourselves the question, "What is my motivation here?" "Is my mood loving" If I am not in a good mood my first priority, before any decisions are made, is to get in a good mood.

I like to remember that my goal is to help my child develop into a loving, self-directed individual. My goal is long term – their personal development, rather than short-term – my peace and quiet.

We can help our children as they carve their path through life by sharing our own experience and learning and also by recognising we can't know what the child's inner guidance is telling them. We can encourage our children to use their feelings as their guide. It is tempting to make every decision for our children and control their behaviour in an attempt to keep them from making mistakes but if we do so we stifle their growth.

How many of us have said, "I told you so" to our children? When our child makes a decision that has unwanted consequences for them we don't need to make them feel worse by pointing out that our advice was correct. We want them to trust their own guidance system rather than be dependent on us. They will learn from their experience in the same way that we do. We can soothe them the way we would soothe ourselves.

For example, a common occurrence is a child choosing not to wear a coat when we know they will need it later. We could choose to carry a coat for them or let them feel the cold a little so they may make a different decision next time when we say it is cold outside. They may want to spend a bit of time outside to get a feel of the temperature so they can decide before you leave for the activity. The approach you take will depend on the circumstances and what will make you feel better. For example, if you have to spend the afternoon outdoors and you know your child will be uncomfortable you might choose to take a coat. If you have the option of heading indoors if your child got too cold you might leave their coat at home. If your child can understand I would tell them what you have decided to do and why.

A recent experience reminded me to allow my children to make their own decisions as much as possible.

I woke early one Saturday morning to help two of my children get ready for a day out with a family friend. The Halloween special event had been booked for ages and I thought they would have a great time playing in the woods with their friends. I was feeling a little rushed for time and was thrown off guard when my 11 year old, Elizabeth, announced that she didn't want to go after all. I became very angry when my gentle then not so gentle encouragement failed to change her mind. I telephoned my friend so she could prepare her little girl who is very fond of Elizabeth and who I knew would be disappointed. Apparently, the little friend was more upset than I had expected and the trip was in danger of being cancelled and that's when I became very angry and upset. I was concerned for my friend's daughter. I was concerned for my other daughter who would be missing out on a day she had been looking forward to. I was worried what my friend would think of my parenting skills, and I was concerned that I was doing the wrong thing by not forcing my daughter to go.

This resulted in lots of crying and shouting (mainly from me) and other members of the family who had become involved. It felt like everything I had learned had gone out of the window. I was a terrible parent. I felt awful and spent the rest of the morning in bed as I was too upset to function.

The first step toward feeling better was remembering that my feeling bad was not an indication that I was bad, but rather an indication that my thoughts were unhelpful. This helped me to calm down and consider how I might think about the situation. Basically, I was still completely acceptable. I wasn't a bad person, just someone trying to do her best. Elizabeth was still completely acceptable. She was just trying to have control over her own life. Nothing had gone wrong.

I remembered toying with the question of how allowing children to make their own decisions by trusting their own guidance system would work in practise. It seemed like I had been given a perfect opportunity to work out the answer.

The conclusions I came to were that firstly I had always put Elizabeth under pressure to be involved in activities as I wanted her to experience everything available. She had often resisted but usually came and ended up enjoying herself. I hated the feeling of my children missing out on something and being disappointed, so I was attempting to avoid this feeling. I decided that even though Elizabeth may have to experience the disappointment of missing an enjoyable event this would be a learning experience for her and it would help her to tune in to her own guidance system. My friend's daughter would be fine without Elizabeth. She had a wonderful time with my other daughter and another little friend.

I also became more convinced that it is more important to listen to our own guidance system than try to please others. I agreed that I would not pressure Elizabeth to attend any events and then she wouldn't be letting people down if she changed her mind as her own guidance system called her more loudly as the event drew nearer.

It highlighted that I had been worrying unnecessarily about Elizabeth and trying to manage her life whereas I could relax and allow her to listen to her own guidance system and face the consequences of her decisions. With seven children in the house it had been draining to try to micromanage their experience so it was a relief to find that I could pass that responsibility and power back to them.

YOUR CHILDREN HAVE THEIR OWN GUIDANCE SYSTEM

"Be yourself, everyone else is already taken."
-Oscar Wilde

I love this little story about my six year old daughter, Grace.

She is a member of the local Rainbow Guides and had been attending for about ten weeks. Because Grace is not a member of the other girls' classes she was finding it difficult to fit in to the group. She is a very popular girl amongst her home-educated friends and other children we spend time with, but it seemed that in this setting the girls were comfortable in their own little groups and didn't want to include Grace.

I had been mildly upset when I was dropping her off and observed her standing alone while waiting for the planned activities to start. I had to remind myself that she was keen to go every week as she was enjoying the activities and I realised she must have known her own worth enough to be unaffected by not being included. We discussed how the girls did not even know her so it couldn't be that they didn't like her and it was probably just that they felt happy in their own groups and didn't feel the need to make more friends. I remember asking her one week if anyone had realised yet how awesome she was.

The last meeting before Christmas was a party. All the girls were told to come in their party dresses. Grace decided to attend in her crocodile fancy dress costume. She had worn it at a fancy dress party at Rainbows previously and, according to Grace, the tail had been the cause of a lot of positive attention for her. I repeatedly tried to persuade her to wear a normal party dress. I said she was already considered unusual because she didn't go to school and this might make it even more difficult to be accepted by the group. She replied that a little girl she had started to play with the week earlier liked her because she was unusual. I decided she would know best what to do.

I had previously thought that six was too young to know what was best but my learning and experience was showing me that each child had their own inner guidance system that I needed to let them follow.

We arrived at the party. Some of the guide leaders looked a little bemused but Grace was immediately surrounded by a group of girls who were interested in her costume and the toy she was carrying. Instead of changing herself to try to please others she had followed her own path with her strong sense of self, who she was, and what her preferences were.

LET YOUR CHILDREN LEARN FROM THEIR MISTAKES

"Anyone who has never made a mistake
has never tried anything new."
-Albert Einstein

I have always argued against this statement. My thinking was, *Why would I let my children make unnecessary mistakes when they can learn from mine?*

On the one hand, time spent with your children discussing, sharing, building a relationship, and listening is all valuable input for them and part of the reason why humans have such a long period of time where they are physically, financially, and emotionally dependant on their parents, and therefore have many opportunities to be guided through all the changes that childhood and adolescence bring. There is a lot of wisdom that can be passed down from one generation to the next. Why let each generation reinvent the wheel, so to speak? Parents have a lot of life experience that they can lovingly share if their children are willing to listen and have respect for their parents' views and life choices.

On the other hand, children will benefit greatly from facing the consequences of their own decisions. As a parent I have found it difficult to see my children being upset as their actions have caused them pain. I have intervened on many occasions only to find that they repeat the action in the future. Of course, there are situations when it is the correct thing to do. My son was convinced he didn't need to heed my advice to stay in the shallow end of the swimming pool without his arm bands. I didn't let him drown! My teenage daughter missing the last bus home has been collected from the bus station with instructions that if it happened again she would be paying for a taxi. In these instances there are no hard and fast rules. Each parent will be more comfortable with a different solution.

A recent incident in our home highlighted to me the importance of a child having to learn from their own mistakes. My sixteen year old daughter Emily has a part-time job cleaning at a local church two or three mornings a week before college. This gives her the pocket money she needs to pay for cinema trips, clothes, concert tickets, and the like. She also does the odd extra job around the house to earn more money. She had expressed that she would like more money with which to buy treats and I had helped her compile a CV and even delivered some to local restaurants and shops for her. A few opportunities had arisen but she wasn't keen on any of them. I said I didn't mind that she didn't take on a job but made it clear I wouldn't be giving her any pocket money now she had turned sixteen. I am not suggesting that this should be a rule in everyone's family, just stressing that she clearly knew what the ground rules were. She had arranged to meet some friends at the local cinema and realised she couldn't afford the entrance fee. On top of that, she had lost her free bus pass earlier in the week, despite me stressing the importance of her putting it back in its holder around her neck rather than in her pocket where she lost it from, so she would have to pay adult bus fare. She was quite upset at not being able to go and I was sorely tempted to give her the money so she could make the trip. However, I knew I would feel resentful if I gave her the money as we had discussed at length her choices about earning money and the importance of looking after her property (she had lost two concert tickets from her pocket the week before). Not only that, she wouldn't learn from her mistakes.

Her sister left for the cinema leaving Emily behind, very upset. At this point I decided the best thing for me to do was to keep out of her way, talk kindly to myself, and think kindly of her. I had to visit an elderly relative later that day and asked Emily if she wanted to join me. I was still consciously thinking positive thoughts and trusting the process. Emily came and though still upset, shared with me that she realised something had to change – either she would have to spend less money or earn more. Also, she was beginning to see the value of being more careful with her belongings. I was glad she had learnt the lesson relatively easily. I had kept out of the equation in that I didn't feel the need to blame or scold or rescue.

We returned home from our relatives only to find that Emily had left her phone behind! What to do? I knew I would have to collect it at some point. We jumped straight back in the car as I had a free hour before another commitment so could easily fit the return journey in. Although nothing was said about the incident Emily had obviously appreciated my efforts and couldn't do enough for me later that day.

HELPING OUR CHILDREN BECOME UNCONDITIONALLY HAPPY

"Unconditional Happiness is the highest technique (to enlightenment) there is."
-Michael Singer

We are not responsible for our children's happiness – they are. This is important to remember when they are in a bad mood. We often end up in a bad mood as well because we think we should be making them happy and therefore feel like we have failed. Also, it is much more pleasant for us to be around happy kids. We often say to them indirectly, "You need to be happy even though you aren't getting what you want e.g. a toy or money, etc. because I can't be happy if I'm not getting what I want (a happy child)."

One of my children loves giving gifts. I had asked her to order some Christmas presents via the internet for herself and her younger siblings and she eagerly agreed. She had ordered herself a few gifts within the budget I had set but had accidentally ordered them using her sister's account so they were being posted to her sister's university address. She had planned to open one of the gifts at a party where Santa would be visiting but it wouldn't be here in time.

She asked could she buy another gift instead but I refused as she already had some gifts under the tree that she could choose from to give to Santa at the party.

She was not impressed and became very sullen. It would have been easy for me to give in to her at that point. A new gift would have been inexpensive and it would have made her happy in the short term. Instead I decided to keep to my plan of her using a gift she already had. She became quite persistent and even more sullen but I could see this was a great opportunity for her to learn unconditional happiness. I didn't want to teach my daughter that she got what she wanted by sulking. I also wanted her to see that she could make herself happy by appreciating what she already had.

I would love to say that she later expressed her love and appreciation for me and recognised my desire for her long term happiness. However she did come to terms with my decision and cheered up.

STAYING HAPPY WHEN OUR CHILDREN AREN'T

"Don't let the behaviour of others destroy your inner peace."
-His Holiness, the Dalai Lama

When I can see that my child is feeling out of sorts I remember my priority is to stay in a good mood. Often this will mean keeping a distance from my child and letting them get their negativity out of their system. Previously, I would rush in to try and make my child feel better but more often than not, I would get drawn into their upset and start to feel bad because I thought my job was to help them feel good. If their mood didn't improve straight away my thoughts would turn negative. I would start judging my capabilities as a mother and then become impatient for them to feel better in order to relieve my discomfort.

Now when my child is in a bad mood I will offer support if they ask for it but as soon as I recognise negative emotions in me I know it is time to leave and find better feeling thoughts. Using my journal and some of the processes I can gain insight into what is bothering me about the situation.

Initially I wondered whether my children would become more negative in order to get my attention, but what I repeatedly find is that they eventually distract themselves and begin to feel better. When they are feeling better they may approach me to discuss what was troubling them but this time they recognise what they want rather than complaining about what is wrong. When they were feeling unhappy they were unable to listen to any suggestions from me anyway and we would both end up frustrated. Often, they don't need my input at all as the 'problem' disappeared as soon as they were in a good mood again.

When my child is having a difficult time, complaining or feeling angry for example, my work is to stay in a good mood and I do this by saying things like, *They will work this out for themselves. I am ready to listen when they are ready to be responsive. It's not the end of the world. They're learning to listen to their own guidance system and finding thoughts to make themselves feel better.*

I can busy myself close by and maybe offer the odd words of comfort such as *I can see that you are upset. I wonder what you will come up with. You will work something out.* The same principle applies when siblings are arguing. Previously the children would have asked for my intervention or I would hurry to find them as soon as I heard raised voices. What I found was firstly, I often didn't know how to sort out the disagreement as I could see that both children had valid points from their perspective, and secondly, each child would become more animated and louder as they tried to convince me that they were right and I should rule in their favour. Now I do not respond to raised voices in another room and the children sort out their disagreements peacefully. If the children approach me I act as a neutral party, listening and maybe offering suggestions, but certainly not casting judgement on either party.

My life is so much calmer now and the children are learning valuable skills and getting on much better with each other and with me. In fact, 99 percent of our interactions are now pleasant and fun.

SIBLING RIVALRY

"My sister and I never engaged in sibling rivalry.
Our parents weren't that crazy about either one of us."
-Erma Bombeck

I have been asked to write about sibling rivalry. It is not something we have had to deal with as a family but I can see how the processes I have shared can easily be used to deal with it.

I would explain to my child that their value is inherent. They do not need to compare themselves to their siblings, or anyone for that matter, to find their value. Their purpose in life is to find what pleases them and do that.

I would remind my child that they do not need my attention or approval in order to feel good. Needing my attention or approval is an indication that they are not giving themselves the approval or compassion they need.

A family is a great place to learn unconditional happiness. People are thrown together that might not otherwise choose to spend time together. This might be especially true in step-families. I tell my children that if they can learn to get along with their siblings then they will be more able to get along with other people. The family can be a great training ground for the rest of life.

My children don't get along all of the time and there are definite personality clashes. I tell my children to give each other space if they are experiencing negative emotion and then discuss the issue (if they feel they need to) when they are feeling calmer. Often they have to agree to disagree. My children know the theory that they are responsible for their own happiness but they are still practising.

When a child is angry or upset with a sibling I ask them to consider what it is they want rather than focusing on what they don't want. They are then in a better position to find a solution.

I soothe myself with the idea that it is normal for siblings not to get along all of the time. I try to stay out of sibling conflict as much as possible. My involvement would often complicate matters. If the subject comes up later I will listen to the child asking for my advice or support and ask them to consider what it is they need I would encourage them to be solution, rather than blame, focused and would encourage them to give their sibling the benefit of the doubt.

As I learn to value myself unconditionally and value my children unconditionally I ensure that I don't add fuel to the fire by favouring one child over another. My children are very different and I find some children easier to get along with than others at times. My work is to practise unconditional love by believing the best of every one of my children and appreciating their unique qualities.

On a lighter note, when one of my children has done something particularly pleasing, or is just fancying a hug, I will whisper to them, *You are my favourite.* They all know that I say it to each one of them individually.

PUNISHMENT OR PREPARATION?

"Rewards and Punishments… are a means of enslaving a child's spirit, and better suited to provoke than prevent deformities."
-Maria Montessori

Clients most commonly seek my help because they are unsure about how to deal with a child's unwanted behaviour. Their efforts up to that point have led to levels of anger and upset in the family that they didn't think were possible. Every relationship in the family is suffering: the relationship between the parents and the child/ren; relationships between parents as they argue over the best way to react to their child's unwanted behaviour; relationships between siblings as everyone is affected by the mood in the family and disputes are not handled in a helpful way.

The purpose of this book is to improve the mood of the reader which will in turn improve the mood in the family home. We have considered the importance of unconditional happiness and the power of finding better feeling thoughts. We have considered how our perception of our role and world view will affect how we undertake that role. For example if we believe that an upset child is 'naughty' then we will respond differently than if see an upset child as 'out of sorts'.

So in response to the questions I am often asked during workshops or 121 coaching sessions I wanted to take this opportunity to elaborate on a few points that I have made in various sections in the book with regards to 'discipline'.

I remember that my child's behaviour is only a symptom of how they are feeling. I focus on their feelings rather than the symptom. I see my child as unhappy rather than naughty. I help them to find ways to be happy rather than punish them.

I remember that my goal is to prepare my child for life outside of the family. In the 'real' world there will be consequences of their mood and behaviour.

I want to help my child learn unconditional happiness. I don't want to teach my child that a temper tantrum will get him what he wants but I do want to respect his feelings. I will have compassion for his bad mood but won't necessarily give him what he wants in order to improve his mood. I used to worry that not giving my child everything they wanted would be limiting for them but now I see that an attitude of appreciation for what they already have is of greater benefit to them.

I want to help him learn responsibility. For example, several years ago, I watched a documentary about families that were having problems with their children's behaviour and were receiving specialist help. One scene has stuck in my mind. A husband and wife were worried about their son, aged around eight, who they felt was unmanageable. The couple watched behind a one-way mirror as their son was asked by a therapist to wash a bowl of dishes. The son refused but the staff would not allow him to leave until the dishes were washed. The son was very strong willed and became very upset at the situation he found himself in. The parent were also upset and announced that they would have given in and not demanded that the child wash the dishes. I know some people will argue with me and feel that the boy shouldn't have been forced to wash the dishes but I remember thinking, *it's only a bowl of dishes.* Of course, the boy could see that if he gave in on this one issue he would have lost a lot of the power he had in his family. In another chapter I describe the benefits of sharing responsibilities in a family. I believe we are a team. I might have more knowledge about a situation and therefore might have to have the final say on occasion, but I endeavour to create an environment where everyone has their needs and preferences met. Several years ago I read a thought provoking book, "With Consent." If I remember correctly, the basic premise is that, in a family, no one has the authority to demand anything from another member. Families would work together to come to mutually satisfactory solutions. Rather than looking for compromises, where everyone can have some of what they want but not all of what they want, the authors suggest families seek common preferences where everyone gets what they want within the natural limitations of the family. I tried to implement the book's ideology for a few days as I did agree with much of what I read, but at the time found it exhausting and unworkable for me. Trying to implement the teachings made me aware of how controlling I was. I realised that I would say *No* to a request because it seemed impossible or too difficult to fulfil but on further consideration would be workable. Even though I didn't follow the principles completely I did start to take the time to hear everyone's opinion fully and work towards a mutually satisfactory solution whenever possible.

I try to remember to ask myself, *what is my motive here?* I also ask, *what is my mood?* My motive should be the long term development of the child rather than a short term fix. I remember that if I am in a bad mood I will not be much help to my child. My priority is to feel better about myself, my child and the situation and then I will be more able to see the solution. When I am in a good mood I do not become part of the problem. As I have been implementing the teachings of this book I have noticed how often I deal with a child's grumpiness with loving humour which often diffuses the situation quickly.

For example, William is my first Neuro-typical boy. He is an energetic, curious and determined little boy. Sometimes he is angry and frustrated. Even at an early age I can see that I will have to intervene more than I ever had to with the girls or with my autistic son. At a play area recently I had to repeatedly pull him away from another little boy whom he was hugging over enthusiastically and becoming frustrated as the little boy ran away. Distraction is a great tool with little ones. My motive is to keep William and his playmates safe and model preferred behaviour, rather than punish. William is quite rough with the family dog but repeated modelling of us gently stroking the dog is paying off. I remind myself that pulling out the drawers in the kitchen so he can climb up them to get on to the kitchen work surface is not naughty but the sign of great intelligence. Nappy changes have been difficult as William does not want to lie still. When I am in a bad mood, nappy changes are fraught and become a battle ground. When I am in a good mood and feeling playful, nappy changes are a time of great fun and interaction.

I treat my child the way I would want to be treated. I give them as much scope to make personal choices as possible but accept that there will always be limitations. When I am in a bad mood, believing that someone or something is stopping me from getting what I want, the last thing I need is someone telling me to change my behaviour. That would inflame me. I need compassion, otherwise known as loving understanding.

I endeavour to stay focused on my child and their needs (and the needs of other that are affected by my child's behaviour) and not care what others think. I am not concerned about others disapproval of me or my child. Try to imagine how this would reduce your stress levels when your child displayed negative emotion in a public place.

I try to be flexible. At times I recognise that my motive for cooperation is just because, *I told you so.* At times like these, I am being stubborn rather than loving. At other times consistency is called for. If my motive is to lovingly guide my child I will feel when I need to back down or be firm.

For example, John, my ten year old boy with autism is strong minded and doesn't like to be told what to do. Personal hygiene isn't one of his priorities. His idea of washing his hands is to put a blob of liquid soap on each palm and then hold his hands under running water. I had showed him many times how to wash his hands properly but he was insisting that his way was good enough. I explained again about unseen germs and the importance of proper handwashing but he was adamant. I decided that this was an issue important enough to insist that he cooperated. I said I would confiscate his Kindle until he washed his hands. The conversation continued for a further 10 minutes or so until I had to take my daughter to the train station. I told John that time was running out as I had to leave in a few minutes. As I was about to leave the house John realised that he wouldn't have his Kindle for half an hour and decided that he would now wash his hands properly. I was tempted to make myself late in order to inspect his washing but realised that he would remember the lesson if he had to wait until I returned.

There will be times when my child can't have or do exactly what they want and this is a great opportunity for them to learn unconditional happiness.

For example, Elizabeth at twelve is often the eldest child at home as her elder sisters are out at college. She has a lot of freedom to do what she pleases when she pleases but there are times when I ask her to do something and she doesn't want to. It is tempting to give in to her complaining but I realise that I am doing no favours if I reinforce the idea that complaining gets her what she wants. Also I do implement consequences. She has the job of washing dishes, wiping down the kitchen work-surfaces and sweeping the kitchen floor. She regularly 'forgets' to sweep or wipe down the work-surfaces. I used to get angry when this happened as it seemed like a simple thing to do. After a discussion with her, we decided upon a consequence. When she didn't do her job completely she would be given an extra job to do. It wasn't long before she was completing her job properly with no reminders from me.

Each parent will have their own unique experience of being faced with behaviour they find unpleasant. I hope I have given you some general principles and examples for you to find new ways of building harmonious relationships between you and your children.

LOVING LIFE

"God gave us the gift of life;
It is up to us to give ourselves the gift of living well."
-Voltaire

APPRECIATION, APPRECIATION, APPRECIATION

"Appreciate again and again, freshly and naively,
the basic goods of life,
with awe, pleasure, wonder and even ecstasy,
however stale these experiences may have become to others."
-Abraham Maslow

Having considered how we can improve our family lives by showing ourselves and our children compassion I want to turn our attention to another way we can improve our parenting journey.

I have a sneaking suspicion that, as a child, I used complaining as a way to get what I wanted because, even as an adult, that was my default setting when I wanted something I thought might be difficult to get. As I began writing this book I realised that writing was an escape for me. The atmosphere in the home was complaining and 'whiny'. I initially thought it was my children's problem and my job was to teach them how to be appreciative. As I became more aware of my thoughts as I used the processes, I realised that my children were learning this habit from me. I have caught myself moaning to my friends about how my kids are always moaning.

I wanted to create a better atmosphere and now I knew that I could not demand appreciation from my children but could model it instead.

When my children are complaining about the one thing they haven't got while not appreciating the one hundred things they have, I know that giving them that one thing they want will not make them happier in the long term. They will simply find something else that they 'need' to make them happy. The same goes for me. I always thought that a new house in the country or a new husband or a new career would give me the joy I was seeking, but I have found that the only thing that needed to change was a change of outlook.

It is easy to take things for granted. I took the children camping last year with a group of friends who also home-educate. We were camped on a muddy field, in cold, wet weather, with compost toilets and cold water to wash dishes in. When we returned home we were all squealing with delight as we turned on lights and switched on electrical appliances. We greatly appreciated the indoor plumbing and hot running water. It wasn't long before we got used to these things again. We would do well to remember all the things we can appreciate rather than focusing on what isn't exactly the way we want it to be.

Upon waking and again at night before sleeping, make a mental or written note of things you appreciate.

MAKE LISTS OF POSITIVE ASPECTS

"Enjoy the little things in life,
for one day you will look back and realise they were the big things."
-Robert Brault

The most useful technique I have found to raise my levels of appreciation, and therefore my happiness, is to write lists of positive aspects. We often take for granted the things that are good in our lives and instead focus on what we think is wrong. Focussing on the positive aspects of various aspects of my life has made me happier than I would have been had I received all the things I thought I needed to be happy. I might have had new people and things in my life, but with a complaining attitude I wouldn't have enjoyed them as much as I could have. Also my happiness would be dependent on those things or people staying around. I have given some personal examples to get you started.

In early 2015 I was feeling a little anxious about money so decided to focus on all the positive aspects of my family's financial position:

> We are living in our own home and are meeting the mortgage payments.
> We have equity in our home.
> This house is big enough to fit all the family in comfortably so we won't need to buy a more expensive house in the future.
> My husband is in secure employment.
> We have always paid our bills and had money left over to pay for life's little luxuries.
> We have pensions and equity in our home when we downsize so we won't need to be concerned about our retirement.
> We have life insurance in case it is needed.
> What is the worse that could happen if we couldn't afford to pay our bills? We might have to cut back or even move to a smaller house but we would be okay.

The best things in life are free.
Time with friends and family or a trip to the park doesn't need to cost anything.

A list of my husband's positive aspects looked like this:

He is trustworthy
He has good morals
He is sociable
He is strong minded and doesn't let me manipulate him (one can imagine how I used to view this characteristic)
He has a good sense of humour
He is hardworking
He works hard to keep fit
He helps to keep the house in good condition
He has lovely dimples and beautiful blue eyes.

We bought our home five years ago because it was big enough to fit my large family in and we could afford it. It is an old farmhouse on the main road and had been used as two shops for the last twenty years. Even though we made the right decision to buy it I had never fully settled here and was always looking for a new place to live. Time spent appreciating my home is time well spent as it spares me lots of negative emotion.

In June 2015 I wrote, 'Things I love about my home:'

Its size comfortably accommodates my large family.
It is in good order.
It is the perfect location for a family with children of lots of different ages to be able to access public transport and local activities and work opportunities.
It has a great layout with good sized rooms.
It is affordable and worth what we paid for it.
We have nice neighbours.
We have a decent sized garden.

At times I have experienced frustration at being a stay-at-home mum. Here is the list of positive aspects that helped me to look at my situation differently:

> I am my own boss and love the flexibility I have.
> I am well provided for by a hardworking husband.
> There is lots of scope for fun with a house full of children aged from twenty to one
> I can create the atmosphere in my home.
> My mood has a massive influence on my family and how well we all get on.
> I love being valued by my children (I need this less these days as I learn to look inside for my value).
> Being a mum is enough. I don't have to do anything else to prove my value. (Before I started to write this book I realised I had to untangle my value from my achievements. I wanted to write for the pleasure of it not to make myself feel more worthwhile).
> There is excitement and adventure within the family .
> I can carve out more time myself to do the things I enjoy that will not have a negative impact on the family.
> Life is meant to be fun.

Create your own lists of positive aspects. If you get stuck for ideas it might be useful to work through the alphabet. The letters X and Z are tricky unless xylophones and zebras play a part in your experience!

A COMPLAINT FREE FAMILY

"If you cannot be positive then at least be quiet."
-Joel Osteen

I recently read an inspiring book called *A Complaint Free World,* which describes the inspiration of Will Bowen, a minister in Missouri, to help solve the problem of chronic complaining and subsequent unhappiness. He handed out wristbands to his congregation that they could use to remind them of any complaining or gossiping they did. They would swap the band from one wrist to another when they recognised a complaint and the challenge was to go for twenty-one days without swapping the wristband from one wrist to another. Apparently the average time it takes to complete the challenge is between five and seven months. The experiment was and still is a huge success with over six million people trying the "Complaint Free Wristband Challenge."

Like most people who tried the challenge I considered myself to be quite an optimistic person but wearing the wristband highlighted to me the amount of complaining I was doing, especially amongst and about my family. I was becoming increasingly conscious of previously unrecognised groans and sighs. I was so glad of the reminder. It was relatively easy to change a complaint into a simple request. Using the ABCDE process I could change my thoughts of annoyance and frustration to thoughts of compassion and understanding.

I had wondered why there was a lot of complaining in my household. Now it was obvious, I was setting the tone and modelling moaning as a way of trying to get what I wanted. I can't stress how quickly the children's attitude improved as they experienced my new way of being.

Wearing the bracelet reminds me to ask for what I want rather than complaining about what I don't want. So, instead of saying, "I am so sick of tidying up after you lot, get in here and put your stuff away." I say something like, "Can whoever has just made a snack please put away everything they have used?"

I try to give other family members the benefit of the doubt, i.e. they aren't purposely leaving lids off jars to annoy me, but they are children, easily distracted, and have different priorities to me. I still mostly ask them to return to replace the lids though. Again, I have to be mindful of my mood and my motive. My desire is not to punish or shame but to teach and share the responsibility for the smooth running of the home.

I haven't yet completed the twenty-one day challenge but I can see the dramatic improvements already. I would highly recommend giving it a go. I just use a stretchy bracelet that can easily be moved from wrist to wrist.

GO GENERAL

"Think less about it if it doesn't feel good."
-Abraham Hicks

Sometimes I am in such a bad mood that I cannot easily find things to be grateful for. If this is the case it is more than likely that I need to sleep. I used to stay up for the fight but now I know that nothing good comes from that. After a nap I feel much more positive and solutions and compassion for myself and others come more easily. If sleeping is not possible I find another way to emotionally or physically back away from the situation that is bothering me. This has been described as 'Going General'. For example, I might go for a walk or go to my bedroom to create some distance between me and the perceived problem. I then have the quiet I need to go general with my thoughts. Rather than focusing on the specific details of the perceived problem I will try and think more general thoughts such as, *in the grand scheme of things this is not a big problem; I love my child so much; things always work out eventually; I have so much that I appreciate; this will pass.* Recognising that the negative emotion is just an unmet need in you can cause you to ask yourself, *what is it that I need or want?*

If I feel able I will explain to my child that I am feeling negative emotion (in whatever way they can understand depending on their age and ability) and that I need some time alone to feel better again. Any conversation with my child while I am feeling out of sorts will not be helpful. Of course, if I decide to stay for the argument then that can be a learning experience for us both. However, the first option is the most pleasant route.

Sometimes you might feel unable to focus on your child at all without feeling negative emotion, so you might want to go even more general and back away from the subject further. For example, the fact that the sun rises every morning (unless you live in the Arctic Circle), the fact that the Earth has been spinning in its orbit in perfect proximity

147

to other planets and you have not had to be concerned about it, the fact that your body has kept itself alive all night while you slept. You can become more specific until you come across a subject that raises negative feelings in you, at which point you can become more general again. So, for example, you might wake in a bad mood so decide to spend a few moments appreciating general things in your universe. You might then get up to use the bathroom and appreciate all the modern conveniences that are at your disposal. You might take a shower and appreciate the warm water on your skin. This might make you think of the large gas bill you have to pay so you can become more general again by reminding yourself that all things are working out for you. You could then appreciate the food you eat at breakfast, the transport you use to travel about in, the people in your life who support you, and so on.

As you move through your day, be aware of as many things as possible that enhance your life experience.

ACCEPT WHAT IS

'God grant me the wisdom
To accept the things I cannot change
To change the things I can
And the wisdom to know the difference'
-Reinhold Niebuhr

A favourite saying of mine is, "It is what it is."

I used to think that 'accepting what is' meant I would have to put up with unwanted circumstances, but a useful analogy has helped me to see what it really means. Imagine driving the car into a ditch. You would want to get out but time spent denying your position, blaming yourself or others, is time wasted. Accepting what is doesn't mean you want to stay there. It just means you accept where you are and look for ways to get out.

I often describe my eighth child William as "my bonus baby." Two years after Charlotte was born I had a miscarriage and then I didn't get pregnant again for what seemed like a long time by my standards. I thought my baby making days were over. Although William was a welcome addition to the family, he was unexpected. I had recently completed a counselling course, become qualified as a life coach, and was in the throes of launching my coaching business when I became pregnant. When William arrived I was still full of ideas and enthusiasm for the business and felt held back by the amount of time spent looking after a newborn baby.

Plenty of times during the writing of this book, I wanted to write but couldn't. At times I became upset and frustrated but I realised that sulking and stamping my feet didn't change anything. In fact, the times when I was frustrated due to my circumstances, were the times when the writing stopped flowing. How could I authentically write about being happy when I felt frustrated? Ironically, when I accepted the fact that I didn't have as much spare time to write and didn't

149

become upset when my writing or planning was interrupted by the baby, the writing flowed again. So instead of huffing and puffing I told myself, *it's no big deal. There is no rush. I can do this another time. It is what it is and moaning won't change it.*

I also considered what things I could change. To help prepare for an unsettled baby I could ensure I rested in the day. If I really wanted to write or had other things I needed to do without interruption I could choose a time when the baby could be happily entertained by his siblings.

MAKING THE BEST OF WHAT IS

"Things turn out best for the people
who make the best of the way things turn out."
-John Wooden

I had the perfect opportunity to practise accepting 'what is' recently. My family and I had been staying at a lovely holiday cottage in South West Scotland. The journey to the cottage had been trouble free and had taken three hours and I expected the return journey to be equally as easy. We set off at 9.30 a.m. and looked forward to returning home in time for lunch.

We had been driving for about five minutes when the car started slowing down. We chugged along for another few minutes before resigning ourselves to the fact that we were going to have to call for breakdown assistance.

Thankfully, we had breakdown insurance and a telephone. We had water and a few snacks in the car so we would be okay for a while. The very nice breakdown man came after about an hour but he couldn't diagnose the problem. He followed us as the car limped along to the next village where we could use a toilet and buy more food.

Because we had seven people in the car a traditional breakdown vehicle couldn't accommodate us. A taxi was called to take us to a town where we could pick up a rental vehicle. The various reactions of the children were enlightening. One child tossed and turned in her seat giving herself a headache while other children were clearly enjoying the adventure. I focused on staying positive. There was nothing I could do to change the situation. I could feel the threat of negativity as we waited longer and longer for the taxi to arrive, but reminded myself that the taxi driver was doing his best to get to us as quickly as possible. We later learnt that he had come out on his day off to collect us. It would have been easy to complain and feel self-pity as I received yet another phone call that things were taking longer than expected.

We had a pleasant drive to the town to collect the rental vehicle but when we arrived the vehicle wasn't ready for us. Again, I had another opportunity to practise appreciation and staying positive. We continued our journey and instead of rushing to get home we took a break at a service station to eat.

We eventually arrived home nine hours after we had left our holiday home.

This episode made me realise that I had forgotten to enjoy the journey of my life and had been rushing to a destination I thought would be better. For example, when the mortgage was paid off and my husband could reduce his hours at work or my baby was a bit older and I could have more free time. Sat in the car waiting I realised that here was as good a place as any to be happy. Complaining wasn't going to change anything and would only make things more difficult.

I wouldn't have chosen to break down but, on reflection, I'm glad we did.

EVERYTHING IS ALWAYS WORKING OUT FOR ME

"Everything happens for a reason and a purpose and it serves you."
-Tony Robbins

My favourite affirmation is *everything is always working out for me.* It is often the first thing I write when I journal. It is so easy to get disheartened when things aren't going the way we want them to and this affirmation keeps me hopeful.

I was planning to run a parenting workshop in Manchester and asked the local newspaper if they would publicise it on their family events page. I was put in touch with a journalist who asked if she could write an article about me and the work I do as a parenting coach and a workshop leader. The article was picked up by a radio station producer who interviewed me for a late night show. I was also asked to record an interview for a television production company.

The workshop didn't run as not enough people booked on to it to cover the room hire cost but I was relieved. In the past I might have been disappointed but remembering that everything is always working out for me kept me focused on the positive. I realised that I had been feeling increasingly uncomfortable at the thought of leaving my nearly one year old with his older sisters for the whole day. They had agreed to look after him and I knew he would have been well cared for but the girls did have other things they would have preferred to do and baby William did like his mum to be available. I realised that I would rather be at home with the children than spending the whole day running a workshop. That was a project I could do when the baby was a little older but if I hadn't planned to hold the workshop I wouldn't have contacted the local newspaper which led to more publicity for this book.

I had almost finished writing this book but had been spending less time on it so I could concentrate on preparing the workshop. I was also wondering how people would find out about the book without me spending hours on social media. Here was the perfect solution. I could write when the children were asleep, do the occasional interview and spread the news of Easy Peasy Parenting much easier than I ever could have imagined.

The workshop not going ahead was not a failure but the perfect outcome.

When things seem to be going wrong or at least not the way you planned, look for the silver lining. Could it be that something even better than you had planned for you and your family could be in its way?

ANOTHER DAY IN PARADISE

*"The real voyage of discovery consists not in seeking new landscapes,
but in having new eyes."*
-Marcel Proust

I recently took the children to a holiday village for a few days. We were all looking forward to a few days of being in the forest and playing in the 'Sub Tropical Swimming Paradise.' I was also hoping to write chapter or two of this book

My fourteen year old usually draws up a chores rota (she loves rotas and lists) but decided that this time one wouldn't be needed as there would be so little to do.

We arrived in the afternoon and after unpacking decided to take advantage of the swimming facilities. A full day of packing, driving, supervising swimming children followed by a late night had left me with a headache. I took the younger children to the park in the morning and on my return found them arguing about who was going to do the dishes. Everyone felt they had done their fair share of the work.

I couldn't believe it. Here we were, in a beautiful location with loads of time to relax and play and the children were complaining about washing a few dishes. Everyone was sulking, including me. The children were sulking because they didn't want to do more than their fair share of the chores, and I was sulking because I wanted everyone to be happy so that I could be happy.

We came up with a simple rota and I made a determined effort to be happy in spite of their mood. After much soul searching I realised that rather than write new chapters for the book I needed to put into practise what I had already written. Even though I knew the theory that it was thoughts rather than circumstances that I needed to work on, a small part of me was still holding on to the belief that if certain factors changed then I would be happier. But here we were, in 'Paradise,' with so much to be thankful for, and yet still we were complaining. I was expecting the children to do what I wasn't doing myself. I was asking them to be appreciative and cooperative so that I could benefit from their good mood and helpfulness.

Why was I finding it so difficult to stay in a good mood and not descend into complaining and self-pity? I think it was because I believed that in order to get what I wanted I had to complain and show people how much I needed their help.

I felt what a lot of parents, especially mothers, feel: guilt. I felt guilty when I asked for help from the children, especially when they were playing, relaxing, or studying. They would regularly complain when I asked for their help, so I had to be extra 'needy' in order to justify my asking.

This insight made me determined to ask for what I wanted and needed without having to show how hard things were for me in order to justify my requests. Everyone in this family contributes to the amount of work that is required to keep things running smoothly so everyone who is able to should contribute.

As well as being more assertive about receiving cooperation with the housework I knew I needed to spend time thinking of the children's positive aspects. Instead of thinking of them as 'spoilt brats' I could recognise that they were right in wanting things to be fair. They have been brought up in an environment where they have had all their basic needs met so asking them to be thankful because they weren't hungry and cold and parentless as some children are wasn't useful for them. Being appreciative is useful in improving our mood but it doesn't mean we have to shoulder more than our fair share of the workload.

I was also thinking of myself as a 'spoilt brat,' asking myself, "Why am I still not happy when I have so much to appreciate?" I realised that my problem wasn't a lack of appreciation but a lack of self-care. I had forgotten another of the aspects that I have written about. I had forgotten to value myself. I had tried to take on more than I should in order to avoid the children's complaints but this had left me feeling overwhelmed and unappreciated. I wanted the children to recognise what I did and willingly offer to lighten my load. When this didn't happen I had to stand up for what I wanted.

A WALK IN THE RAIN

"Life isn't about waiting for the storm to pass.
It's about learning to dance in the rain."
-Author unknown

I decided to take a walk with Charlotte, aged four. She usually loves a little walk around the block, especially if it ends in a visit to the local shop for a treat. It was winter and the sun would only last for another hour or so. Charlotte had just awoken from a nap and was a little grumpy. By the time she was dressed for the cold weather and we had left the house it had started to gently rain. Charlotte was not happy and I had a choice. Do I allow negative thoughts to set the tone for our trip or do I look for a positive slant? I could have regretted that I woke her up to bring her out for a walk. I could have questioned my decision to come out at all. We could be snuggled up together in the warmth of our home. These thoughts would have been valid but they were not helpful. If I had not challenged these gently negative thoughts I could have ended up in a bad mood. There would then have been a high probability that I would take my bad mood out on Charlotte who was complaining. Instead, I decided to soothe myself and try to soothe Charlotte. We had waterproof coats on. The shop wasn't far away. There were puddles to splash in. The flowers were getting a drink. The thought that brought the biggest smile to my face was that here was a perfect opportunity to model to my child happiness in the face of contrast. I realised that I would rather have this opportunity than be walking in glorious sunshine. We had been inside all day and chose to take a walk just as the rain began. I might have thought that I was a very unlucky person but eventually I came to the conclusion that I was very blessed.

CAN'T SOMEONE ELSE CHANGE FOR A CHANGE?

"We cannot change others but when we change ourselves
we may end up changing the world."
Melody Beattie

Sometimes it feels exhausting to keep looking for the positive aspects in a situation or person. I had been practising these processes for over a year when I had another period of feeling angry and frustrated. I was fed up of always giving people the benefit of the doubt while everyone else just did whatever they pleased. At times it seemed as though nothing was improving and people were still as uncooperative as they had always been. I later realised that there had been improvements but in my bad mood I couldn't see them and I had reverted back to wanting people to change to please me. I had been using the processes to try to manipulate people rather than be genuinely unconditionally happy.

One weekend was particularly explosive. I was more tired than usual as the baby was teething and not sleeping well. I was looking for support from other people to help me get the rest I needed rather than cutting back my schedule. Everyone I was looking for support from had genuine reasons why they couldn't help and I was frustrated.

I went for a walk with my husband and shouted and cried and complained for most of the journey. My husband listened patiently but by the end of the walk I knew more clearly than ever that it was my responsibility to be in a the best mood I could by looking after myself and being appreciative. This felt like a last ditch attempt to control others in order to make my life the way I wanted it to be but I could see the futility of it.

LOOKING FORWARD

"The best way to predict your future is to create it."
-Abraham Lincoln

HAPPINESS IS A WORTHWHILE GOAL

"Happiness is the meaning and the purpose of life,
the whole aim and end of human existence."
-Aristotle

I hope I have convinced you that the best thing I can do for my children is be happy and I hope I have given you enough tools to help create happiness in the midst of family life. Now I want to take this one step further by doing some exercises I learnt as a life coach.

For many years of parenting my sense of achievement – and therefore value – was tied up with how clean and tidy the house was, or how many activities I had done with the children, or what I had achieved that day, or how happy the children were.

The problem was that I would wake up in the morning to a messy house because I had fallen into bed the evening before feeling too grumpy and exhausted to tidy up. I would spend what seemed like all day, tidying up, washing dishes, preparing meals, spending time with the children, or taking the children to and from various activities.

By the time my husband Bill came home from work there was a cooked meal ready for him, but the house looked no different than when he had left for work in the morning. I was looking for appreciation from Bill because I underestimated my contribution and wanted reassurance. When pressed he would say he appreciated what I did, but comments such as, "When was the last time you cleaned the fridge?" would send me into a rage. He didn't mean any harm, but he had been brought up to do jobs around the house on a regular basis. For example, in his house the fridge would be cleaned weekly.

Also, although there were many happy moments, the children were sometimes unhappy and I would take this personally, feeling I had failed at reaching another of my goals, which was to have happy children.

One thing I could control was taking the children to activities. We home-educate our children so taking them to educational or social activities is a part of my responsibility. I would take the children to activities that, looking back, they weren't bothered about attending. Going out gave me a sense of achievement but it left me feeling overwhelmed as time out of the house meant I had less time to do the household chores. Nowadays, we still attend activities, but not so many and for different reasons. We go out to learn or to have fun rather than for me to feel like I am doing a good job.

Not valuing my achievements in a day meant I would try to fit too much in. I didn't feel like I could take a break as that way I wouldn't meet any of my goals. Or so I thought. If I was doing housework I felt I should be giving the children my attention. If I was playing or working with the children then I was bothered by the jobs I wasn't accomplishing.

Looking back I can see that my goals were not helpful.

HOW DOES YOUR IDEAL LIFE LOOK?

"The deepest secret is that life is not a process of discovery,
but a process of creation.
Seek therefore not to find out who you are,
seek to determine who you want to be."
-Neale Donald Walsch

I had been trying to meditate regularly but, due to constant interruptions, often left a 'meditation' session more frustrated than if I'd not even tried. During the middle of one meditation session my toddler came in to the room and climbed onto my lap, book in hand. Previously I might have been frustrated that my goal of meditation was not being accomplished. Then I had a wonderful revelation. I realised that although my goal was to meditate, my ultimate goal was to be happy. Getting angry or frustrated with him was not meeting my greater goal of happiness. I sat and read with him for a few minutes before he toddled off and I could continue my quiet time.

So let's spend time setting some realistic, helpful goals.

Spend some time imagining how you would like your family to look. Not physically but how you interact and thrive together and individually. Some people like to do this in pictures and others find creating word pictures easier.

The idea is to come up with a statement or goal that describes the aspect of your family life that you are considering, the way you want it to be.

The goal should be:

Stated in the positive

Very often we complain about what is wrong without considering what we do want. Because our mind works in pictures it cannot form an image of what we don't want. It needs to know what we do want so it can form a picture of that. Our goals might be general, such as, *I am more peaceful,* or specific, such as, *I am home in time for tea every evening.*

Within your control

Don't let achieving your goal be dependent on the support, goodwill or agreement of others. You can only control yourself. You will find that the behaviour of others does adapt to your changed behaviour but you must stay focused on the management of your behaviour only. For example, *my children are always respectful,* is not under your direct control so it is not an ideal goal statement. A better statement would be *I am respectful to my children.*

Described in as much detail as possible

The more detailed you can make your goal or desired state then the easier it is for you to focus on and therefore create. Often we can't imagine the details of our ideal life but we know how we want to feel. As we focus on the feeling, the details will fill in.

In harmony with your values

Your goals for you and your family need to be in harmony with your purpose and your other goals. You will subconsciously sabotage any goals that are not in keeping with your core values.

Stated in the present tense

The mind works in the present. Talking as if your goal is already achieved will mean you will line up with that reality more easily. Phrasing it in the future tense keeps your goals always out of reach.

Other factors that will help you reach your goals.

Research shows that sharing your goals with other supportive people helps you to achieve them. Don't share your vision of your ideal family life with people who might discourage you.

Thinking about all the benefits of achieving your goals has been proven to help in achieving them. Don't spend time focusing on what might happen if you don't achieve them.

Reward yourself for making progress toward your goals. You will find that moving toward your dream family life is a reward in itself.

Here are a few examples of Family Goals that you might find useful.

I am aware of my feelings and do what I can to feel good more of the time.
I stay upbeat more often even when family members are experiencing negative emotion.
Each family member spends time doing things that please them.
I prioritize getting in a good mood before acting.
I appreciate the members of my family and focus on their positive aspects.
The family has fun together and relaxes together.
I show myself and other family members, compassion more of the time.
Everyone contributes fairly to the running of the home.

FOCUS WHEEL

"If you always do what you've always done,
you'll always get what you've always got."
-Henry Ford

A slightly different angle to goal setting that I have discovered is the Focus Wheel. It can be used to improve my mood by helping me to focus on what I want rather than what I don't want. It also helps me to focus on factors that are under my control.

The idea is to think about what you want and then find thoughts that support this statement. For example, on a recent camping holiday I was feeling overwhelmed as I hadn't had a break from the children. They seemed to be complaining a lot, and on reflection, so was I. I recognised that I needed some time out so I left the children with my sixteen year old daughter and took myself away to a quiet spot to do a focus wheel and get myself in a good mood again.

It took several attempts before I settled on a workable goal. My first attempt was *I want the children to be thankful and cooperative.* I realised that this wasn't an ideal goal as I couldn't change the children by focusing on their behaviour. I could only change my behaviour by changing my thoughts and only then might the children's mood and behaviour change. My second attempt was that we would all be happy all the time. Again, I realised that I was including the children's improved behaviour in my focus wheel thus leaving my mood dependant on external circumstances. Also, being happy all the time was unrealistic. I settled on the third attempt, which was, *I want to feel peaceful and joyful around my children.* This statement gave me full control of my mood independent of external circumstances. Writing the statement in the present tense gave me the focus statement, *I am peaceful and joyful around my children.*

I placed this statement at the centre of the page and began to look for thoughts that would help me achieve this goal. I wrote them all around the outside of the central goal statement. The statements I wrote included: *I accept that my children are never going to behave perfectly because no one is "perfect" in the sense that none of us are unconditionally loving all the time; my role is to love them unconditionally; I am most beneficial to my children when I am feeling good so I will make regular time to find positive thoughts and therefore feel good; having children is great practise for having unconditional joy and growing as a person; my happiness can be independent of external circumstances; I can choose to focus on their strengths and appreciate them being in my life; my children are like a mirror, reflecting my own mood back to me. I am therefore glad they have shown me that I was being complaining and unappreciative; I am glad that I can recognise when I am not feeling happy because I can then make time to change my thoughts.*

The whole process must have taken only ten minutes but it changed the course of the rest of the day. For me, the most helpful part of the process is focusing on what I want rather than what is going wrong.

CHALLENGING LIMITING BELIEFS

"Believe you can and you're halfway there."
-Theodore Roosevelt

Each of us will have hundreds, if not thousands of unconscious beliefs that govern our lives. Limiting beliefs are those, often unrecognised beliefs that keep us from achieving our goals and vision for ourselves and our family.

Regular journaling will help you to recognise recurring thoughts that are holding you back from the life you want.

For example, *There is never enough time; We are always late; We never have enough money; I can't work and give my children the attention they need; I have to work outside the home to raise enough money for us to live comfortably; It will always be this way.*

Each of us will have different limiting beliefs. The limiting belief that I uncovered at a life coaching seminar was *I need to be available for my children 24/7 in order for them to thrive.*

The powerful method to challenge limiting beliefs is so simple you might find it difficult to believe, but I promise you it works and I encourage you to try it. Your mind just needs a new way to see your situation.

So what is this simple yet powerful method? Rewrite the exact opposite of your limiting belief. For example, I changed my statement to *I don't need to be available for my children 24/7 in order for them to thrive.* You could call this an enhancing belief. Up until this point every time I would do something without my children or for myself I would feel guilty. Now I can pursue my own interests as well as fulfil my role as a mother. I am more fulfilled and I have found it to be true that my children don't need my attention 24/7. In fact, I think they prefer the fact that I am not constantly focusing on them.

What limiting beliefs do you have that are affecting your parenting?

Write the limiting belief and then it's opposite.

As you move in the direction of the life you want, more limiting beliefs will be activated and exposed. For example, if your belief is that your value is related to how hard you work and you decide to take my advice and enjoy yourself more, this limiting belief will become more apparent. This belief will make you feel uncomfortable and you might be tempted to step back into your comfort zone of working hard to feel valuable. Journalling and processing your thoughts using one of the processes I have shared with you will help you to avoid stepping back into an unhelpful pattern of behaviour.

POSITIVE AFFIRMATIONS

"All that we are is the result of what we have thought."
-Buddha

I find it invaluable to repeat positive affirmations to myself. You might like to write down your favourite ones and put them around your home or work or in your diary. When I find myself ruminating over a negative thought, having a positive statement to replace it is necessary. If I try to ignore the negative statement it keeps returning like a bothersome fly. I need a positive statement in order to replace it. Often I will write out a particular statement several times in my journal until I really start to feel it. Some of our limiting beliefs are so entrenched in our minds that it takes many episodes of using positive affirmations before we can change our thoughts completely.

Here are some of my favourites:

Everything is working out for me
Life is meant to be fun
Life is a gift, not a test
Life is meant to be enjoyed, not endured
I breathe deeply
Life is not about avoiding the storms but learning to dance in the rain
Happiness is an inside job
It is what it is
I am where I am
The time to be happy is NOW
Happiness is a journey, not a destination
My feelings are my guide
Get in a good mood then...
Practise feeling how I think I will feel when I have what I want
I am acceptable and valuable NOW
There is nothing I need to do to be more valuable
My value is inherent

I deserve compassion
No one is perfect so I can't expect perfection from myself
I am doing my best
Others are doing their best
I am doing extremely well
Appreciate, appreciate, appreciate
I am solution focused (I trust that there is a solution)
I head towards the life I want with positive thoughts
I do something every day to bring me closer to my dreams
I tell the story I want to live
Everything is always working out for me.

A TWIST IN THE TALE

*"Choose a job you love
and you will never have to work a day in your life."*
-Confucius

Before I became pregnant with my last baby, William, I had qualified as a life coach and was looking forward to starting a business and working part-time outside the home. I had always wanted to be a stay-at-home mum but after 20 years felt ready for a change.

It was around the same time that I came across the philosophy I am sharing with you, namely that being unconditionally happy is a worthwhile goal. I was eager to share the ideas that were helping me and my family so much and so began writing this book. I thought that writing this book would give me something to do while William was a baby and my career as a life coach was on hold.

As I was journaling and writing the book it became increasingly apparent that my desire to work outside the home was more about escaping the difficulties of my family life than moving toward a new challenge. I discovered I had a lot more negative emotion about my circumstances as a stay-at-home mum than I realised.

As I used the processes on a daily basis to change my negative thoughts and challenge limiting beliefs I began to enjoy my home life increasingly, to the point where I no longer wanted to work outside the home. I had planned to deliver a parenting workshop when William was 11 months old and was relieved when it couldn't go ahead. At that point I realised that writing, rather than coaching, suited me and my desire to be with my children.

I did need a new challenge and an outlet to express my creativity and writing gives me the best of both worlds.

I understand that many mums enjoy working outside the home or have to work to pay the bills but I have spoken to mums who work as an escape from the children. My hope is that this book will empower mums to make choices about how they spend their time from a place of doing what they want rather than avoiding what they don't want. My hope is that mums have a balanced, joyful life, doing as many things as possible that please them.

REFERENCES AND BIBLIOGRAPHY

Ben-Shahar, T. PhD. "Happier. Can You Learn To Be Happy?" (2008) McGraw Hill

Bowen, W. "A Complaint Free World" (2007) London: Virgin Books Ltd

Chapman, G. (1992) "The Five Love Languages: How To Express Heartfelt Commitment to Your Mate." Chicago: Northfield Publishing.

Cooper, D. "Light Up Your Life. Discover Your True Purpose and Potential" (1995) London: Piatkus Publishers Ltd

Crane, P.J. PhD. "Ordering From the Cosmic Kitchen. The Essential Guide to Powerful, Nourishing Affirmations" (2002) California: The Crane's nest

Davies, W. "Overcoming Anger and Irritability. A Self-Help Guide Using Cognitive Behavioural Techniques." (2008) UK: Constable and Robinson Ltd

Fredrickson, B.L. PhD. "Love 2.0. Creating Happiness and Health in Moments of Connection" (2013) New York: Plume

Fredrickson, B.L. PhD. "Positivity" (2009) London: Oneworld Publications

Hicks, E. and J. "The Astonishing Power of Emotions. Let Your Feelings Be Your Guide." (2007) Hay House, Inc.

Hopgood, M-L. "How Eskimos Keep Their Babies Warm. Parenting Wisdom From Around the World." (2013) London: Macmillan

Keller, J. "Attitude is Everything. Change Your Attitude and You Change Your Life" (1999) London: Catalyst

Kundtz, D. "Stopping. How To Be Still When You Have To Keep Going." (1999) Dublin: Newleaf

Seligman M.E.P. PhD. "Learned Optimism. How To Change Your Mind and Life" (1990) Free Press

Tolle E. "The Power of Now. A Guide to Spiritual Enlightenment.' (1999) UK: Hodder and Stoughton

Wiseman, R. Prof. "59 seconds. Think A Little, Change A Lot." (2009) London: Macmillan

SERVICES AND SOCIAL MEDIA

INDIVIDUAL COACHING

I am available for 1 2 1 coaching in person or over Skype or Facetime. Many parents appreciate the opportunity to share their concerns in a private setting. By listening carefully I can help uncover the limiting beliefs that are keeping you from experiencing the family life you desire.

FAMILY COACHING

Your very own SuperNanny (but without the naughty step). I am happy to spend time with you to coach you gently and lovingly into more enjoyable ways of interacting with each other. This can be repeated several times until you feel ready to 'go it alone.'

WORKSHOPS

I regularly run workshops based on the philosophy that has changed my life so much. In a group we explore many techniques shared in this book that can easily be used to bring the joy back into your parenting journey. Previous workshop attendees have enjoyed the camaraderie amongst the parents and hearing other's experiences has reminded them that they are not alone. Workshops are either held over a full day or over several sessions depending on your requirements and location. Please get in touch to discuss holding a workshop near you. I am based in the North West of England but will travel if necessary (especially to exotic locations).

STAFF TRAINING

I offer staff training sessions for those working with children and families. Nursery and School staff often ask me how they can best work with parents to support the children they care for. During a training session we discover how an attitude of compassion for ourselves and others is the most conducive to harmonious working relationships. We then explore in more detail how we put this into practice in a nursery or school setting. Attendees leave with lots of practical ways of increasing their own happiness, encouraging the parents they work with to be happier and improve their working relationship with parents.

PUBLIC SPEAKING

I have experience of public speaking and am happy to address groups on the subject of parenting. If you would like me to address a group of parents, expectant parents, grandparents or those dealing with children or parents, such as nursery or school staff, please get in touch.

easypeasyparent@gmail.com

www.easypeasyparenting.co.uk

SOCIAL MEDIA

I would love to connect with you on Social Media

Easy Peasy Parenting on Facebook, Instagram and YouTube.

Easy Peasy Parent on Twitter.

77792496R00099

Made in the USA
Columbia, SC
05 October 2017